THE
NOT TERRIBLY GOOD
BOOK OF
HEROIC FAILURES

An intrepid selection from the
original volumes

STEPHEN PILE

FABER & FABER

First published in 2012
by Faber & Faber Limited
Bloomsbury House
74–77 Great Russell Street
London WC1B 3DA
This paperback edition first published in 2019

Typeset by Faber & Faber Limited
Printed and bound by CPI Group (UK) Ltd, Croydon, CRO 4YY

The right of Stephen Pile to be identified as author
of this work has been asserted in accordance with Section 77
of the Copyright, Designs and Patents Act 1988

A CIP record for this book
is available from the British Library

ISBN 978-0-571-35289-0

FSC
www.fsc.org
MIX
Paper from
responsible sources
FSC® C020471

2 4 6 8 10 9 7 5 3 1

To all those who have written terrible books on how to be a success, I dedicate this terrible book on how it's perfectly all right to be incompetent for hours on end because I am and so is everyone I know.

CONTENTS

'If a thing's worth doing, it's worth doing badly.'
G. K. CHESTERTON

INTRODUCTION

Here we are again. Happy as can be. All good friends and ready for a quick trot round the archive.

It is quite a thing really, but I have spent much of my adult life collecting stories of comic catastrophe, like a lepidopterist with a net or a trainspotter outside an engine shed. One day somebody said, 'They are heroic failures, aren't they?' And the label stuck. This interest all began with a club.

It is a measure of my obsession that over thirty-two years I have compiled enough evidence to write not one, not two, but three books on this mighty subject.

In 1977 I formed the Not Terribly Good Club of Great Britain. To get into it you had to be not terribly good at something, proud of it and willing to give a brief talk on or demonstration of your area of incompetence at our occasional meetings.

There was a Salon des Incompetents, an exhibition of our inspiringly sub-standard artwork, and there was also a regatta with only one air bed, which made the races less hotly competitive than they need have been. At these meetings people would say 'Have you heard about the world's worst bullfighter?' And my collecting days had begun.

Before long I was the Norris McWhirter of under-achievement. What he did for the biggest, the fastest and the best as editor of *The Guinness Book of Records*, I did for my sort of person on the other side of the fence, recording and revering the sheer surreal genius of the worst, the slowest and the least successful

The first *Book of Heroic Failures* was a heartfelt counterblast to the all-pervading success ethic in Western culture. Success, it argued, is overrated and Man's real genius lies in quite the opposite direction. Being really bad at something requires skill, panache, style and utter individualism. That book sang the praises of the worst in every sphere, people who are so bad at their chosen endeavour that their names shine like beacons for future generations.

Here were the immortal Carolino, who wrote the world's worst phrasebook, the abysmal El Gallo, the worst ever bullfighter, and the dire Foster-Jenkins, whose singing was so appalling that she packed Carnegie Hall with admirers.

At the time none of us dreamt that there could ever be a second volume. Humanity had surely reached the frontiers of what was possible in our field. Could anyone hope to match the immortal Nuttall, an explorer with no sense of direction whatsoever, who was perpetually lost? Could anyone surpass the world's worst tourist, Nicholas Scotti, who spent two days in New York thinking he was in Rome? Would anybody ever break the record for the smallest audience for a live theatrical show (one)?

The answer, we now know, is yes. *Homo sapiens* had moved onwards downwards to ever more glorious feats.

It would be another twenty-five years before the *Ultimate Book of Heroic Failures* was completed in 2011, suggesting that there really is no limit to what is possible, but the present volume combines the high spots of the first two books. Here for the first time in one set of covers are some of the early all-time greats. Here are the great names: Robert 'Romeo' Coates, the world's worst actor, and the Cherry Sisters whose variety act was so bad that the law of libel had to be changed so theatre critics could describe their performance without fear of litigation.

The first *Book of Heroic Failures* was designed as the club's official handbook. When it appeared in the best-seller list I was thrown out as president, having brought shame on the membership.

In only a few months the club had received twenty thousand enquiries from members of the public wishing to join. And so in 1979 the club disbanded on the grounds that it was now a roaring success. Even as failures, we failed.

For the next decade my passion for this subject continued unabated. The *Return of Heroic Failures* came out to mark the tenth anniversary of the first book, but due to a mathematical error it appeared only nine years afterwards.

Connoisseurs among you will know, for example, that 1980 was a vintage year. It brought an incredible outburst of achievement to admire and savour. It warrants a whole chapter of its own.

Elsewhere, it had been a decade of solid achievement. The cultural sphere had seen amazing creativity while the criminal mind once again surpassed itself with a consistently high level of performance.

We also had to applaud the huge growth of activity in the United States of America, which lagged behind for so many years but shot ahead with more entries than any other part of the world. Given its size and tremendous natural resources, there is no reason why this still-young country should not lead the field in time and make a genuine contribution to our subject. The Soviet Union also made its first entry with the least successful wedding toast on record.

As it happens, this is my last ever word on the subject of heroic failure and I have written a whole farewell address, but you cannot have that sort of thing in an introduction. Good heavens, no. This is the last place you want philosophical reflection so I have hired a small van and driven it round the back of the book to deposit in the epilogue.

How to Read This Book

This history is divided up into manageable chunks of information. The best thing is to use it like a swimming pool – dip in occasionally, but come out quickly and lie somewhere, exhausted, with a strong drink.

Before we set off on our conducted tour around some pretty inspired fallibility, awarding wooden spoons wreathed in a laurel, it remains only to echo the words of the Philaster Chase Johnson while encouraging readers to plough through his magazine article in 1920:

'Cheer up, the worst is yet to come.'

1

NEW WORLD RECORDS

'The last shall be first.'
Matt. 19:30

The Smallest Audience

In August 1980 Joan Melu, a Romanian folk singer, broke all existing records for the smallest ever audience. Effortlessly pushing aside the previous contenders, he drew an audience of none whatsoever for a concert of what he described as his own style of country and western.

Arriving on stage at the Capitol Theatre, Melbourne, in dark glasses and casual clothing, he gazed down on the 2,200 empty seats and gave a two-hour show, which overran by 30 minutes due to encores.

Mr Melu performed throughout as if people were there. Coming back on stage after a 15-minute interval, the singer announced over the speaker system, 'Ladies and gentlemen, Joan Melu.' Towards the end of the performance he asked, 'Hey, everybody, do you want to hear my new one?'

After the show he said that he was 'a little nervous' beforehand, but felt very satisfied with the way it had gone. 'I love this life,' the artist commented.

According to a stagehand, Mr Melu perched on a stool one metre from the edge of the stage and did not move for two hours except to strum his guitar and mumble into the microphone in an attractively monotone fashion. 'Every song appeared the same, musically and vocally,' he enthused.

Explaining his art, the singer said that he does not pay too much attention to the music because 'life is in the song not the notes'.

Oxford and Cambridge Boat Race Sinkings

In the annual boat race between the universities of Oxford and Cambridge on the River Thames in London the crews were neck and neck until 1983, having each sunk three times.

Cambridge pioneered the art in 1857, but Oxford showed their mettle in 1925 and again in 1951. The most recent demonstration was by Cambridge in 1978.

The greatest ever Oxford and Cambridge boat race was the memorable 1912 contest in which both boats sank.

Oxford went under first and made for the riverbank. Once the boat had been emptied of water, they could not restart because one of their oarsmen had disappeared into the crowd to chat with a friend. Some while later he returned and told his disbelieving crewmates that it was 'my chum Boswell'.

Oxford then saw Cambridge go by, but they were swimming and their boat was nowhere visible. Sadly, this fine race was abandoned just as it was getting interesting.

In 1984 Cambridge took a 4–3 lead when they achieved the unique distinction of sinking before the race began. Twenty minutes before the start they rowed into a moored tug and split their own boat in half. Full of admiration, the race umpire, Mr Michael Sweeney, observed, 'The cox is only small and he is sitting behind big men. He must have been unsighted.'

The Fastest Failure of a Driving Test

Until recently the world record was held by Mrs Helen Ireland of Auburn, California, who failed her driving test in the first second, cleverly mistaking the accelerator for the clutch and shooting straight through the wall of the driving test centre.

This seemed unbeatable until 1981 when a Lanarkshire motor mechanic called Thompson failed the test before the examiner had even got into the car. Arriving at the test centre Thompson hooted the horn to summon the examiner, who strode out to the vehicle, said it was illegal to sound your horn while stationary, announced that Thompson had failed and strode back in again. Genius of this kind cannot be taught. It is a natural gift.

The Worst Boxing Debut

In February 1977 Mr Harvey Gartley became the first boxer to knock himself out after 47 seconds of the first round of his first fight before either boxer had landed a punch.

It happened in the regional bantamweight heats of the fifteenth annual Saginaw Golden Gloves contest in

Michigan, when our man was matched against Dennis Outlette. Neither boxer had fought in public before. Both were nervous.

Mr Gartley started promisingly and came out of his corner bobbing, weaving and dancing. As the crowd roared them on, he closed in, threw a punch, missed his opponent, whacked himself on the jaw and saw stars. The referee counted him out.

The Worst Homing Pigeon

This historic bird was released in Pembrokeshire in June 1953 and was expected to reach its base that evening.

It was returned by post, dead, in a cardboard box, eleven years later, from Brazil. 'We had given it up for lost,' its owner said.

The Most Misspelt Name

Edward A. Nedelcov of Regina in Canada smashed all records with an amazing 1,023 misspellings of his family name since January 1960. He finds that Nevelcove, Neddlecough, Middlecou and Needochou are quite common versions. However, a letter from the Club Med improved on these by writing to Edward Nedle and Co. His bank addressed him once as Needleco and later as Nedleson. Even a telegram from a close friend in Sydney accepting a wedding invitation was addressed to B. Heddlegove.

On a receipt for nine extra-large spare ribs from Western Pizzas he was down as Meerinwoz. On a later receipt for nine extra-large chickens he was Petlecode. A third receipt said Nidcole and a fourth, Nuddlecale. At this point he switched to Romano Pizzas who went for Nettlecove.

As a primary school teacher, he has now taken to including his own name in spelling tests. Amid 'cat', 'bread', and 'please' he inserts 'Mr Nedelcove' with universally wayward results. Kevin Seivewright got it down as Mr Nettlecoke while in her class diary Lisa Mae Clarke wrote, 'Today I started at Mabel Brown School. I am in room number one and my teacher's name is Nevelcod.'

He once wrote to the Queen telling her about his grade-seven children. His proudest possession is a reply from her Majesty addressed to 'E. A. Dedelcov'.

The Least Successful Pigeon Race

Nothing brings greater excitement to a pigeon race than the complete disappearance of all or most of the competitors. In 1978, 6,745 birds were released at Preston in Lancashire. Of these, 5,545 were never seen again amid rumours that they had retired to the Devonshire coast.

'In all my forty years with racing pigeons,' said Mr James Patterson, Secretary of the Ayrshire Federation of Homing Pigeons, 'I have never known anything like it. They have vanished. Someone suggested they might have flown over a grouse moor and been shot. I can't believe they could have got all 5,545.'

This record, however, was comprehensively shattered in 1983 when the Northern Ireland Pigeon Racing Society lost 16,430 in one go. Although a handful of duller birds flew straight home in record time, swarms of more adventurous little creatures were later found basking in country gardens all over West Wales. Housewives were asked to leave out rice, lentils and dried peas to build the birds' strength up but, eventually, special transport was laid on for the journey home.

The Most Overdue Library Book

It has long been thought that the most overdue book in the history of library services was Dr J. Currie's *Febrile Diseases*, which was taken out of the University of Cincinnati Medical Library in 1823 by Mr M. Dodd and returned by his grandson 135 years later.

In fact, this feat was shot to ribbons by a Bishop of Winchester. In 1650 he borrowed the aptly named *Book of Fines* from Somerset County Records Office. A register of property transactions in Taunton between 1641 and 1648, this volume so enthralled the bishop that it remained in his office for two hundred years. It then passed to the Church Commissioners who hung onto it for another century or so.

In 1985 the book was returned to Somerset County Library, having accrued a fine of approximately three thousand pounds.

The Fastest Knockout

Ralph Walton's fine record of being knocked out in ten and a half seconds lasted only a year and six days so intense is the competition. On 4 November 1947 Pat Brownson saw stars after the first and only punch of his contest against Mike Collins.

This rather special boxer actively contributed to only four seconds of the Golden Gloves Tournament in Minneapolis, Minnesota. He was so far beyond encouragement that they dispensed with the traditional count of ten.

The Least Successful Learner Driver

Now that Mrs Miriam Hargrave, the world record holder, has let us all down by passing her driving test at the fortieth attempt, the field becomes wide open for a promising newcomer. Many doubters felt, however, that her dazzling total of 212 lessons would be unsurpassed. Oh ye of little faith . . .

By March 1980 the sprightly Mrs Betty Tudor of Exeter had been learning for nineteen years and clocked up a breathtaking 273 lessons. In this time she had nine instructors and was banned from three driving schools. She put in for only seven tests and failed them all with flying colours.

The seventh ended when she drove the wrong way round a roundabout, whereupon the examiner screamed at her and said that he would drive from then on. Mrs Tudor told him that 'if it hadn't been for the cars coming in the opposite direction, hooting, he wouldn't have noticed anything wrong'.

Although Mrs Tudor has now decided to sell the car, one suspects that she is only resting. You cannot keep a talent of that magnitude down for long.

The Most Rejected Book Manuscript

When we last heard of Mr Gilbert Young, his book, *World Government Crusade*, had been rejected by more publishers than any other manuscript, having been returned 105 times. 'A copy seems to come back every day,' he said in 1973, shortly before writing to the Soviet ambassador asking if a Russian publisher might be interested.

They were not; and nor were a further 99 British publishers. This brings his total to an almost unbeatable 205 rejection slips, all of which he keeps as souvenirs.

'I am running out of publishers to try,' observed Mr Young, a retired insurance official, whose book outlines the policies of the World Government and Old Age Pensioners Party that he founded in 1958. His main scheme is to establish one government for the whole world with one police force and one compulsory language. Another of his ideas is to turn Buckingham Palace into an old folks' home.

The Fastest Defeat in Chess

Gibaud has been overthrown. Ever since 1924 this French chess master has been revered for achieving defeat in only four moves. A Monsieur Labard played the walk-on part in this great scene.

But in the 1959 US Open Championship somebody called Masefield was a useful foil, moving around the white pieces in a match that enabled the immortal Trinka to be checkmated in three moves:

1. P–K4   P–KN4
2. N–QB3 P–KB4
3. Q–R5 *mate*

The Least Successful Garage

The previous record holder merely had a garage with four steps up the front. However, in a fearless advance in garage design Mrs Caroline Hitchens decided to incorporate one in the basement of her dream home built on a hillside in Penzance.

Any car parked in this garage would have needed to cross the lawn and several flowerbeds and then descend a thirty-foot cliff to the road. To get out at the back of the house the car would have to burrow up through thirty feet of earth to join the traffic.

The Least Successful Defrosting Device

Mr Derek Davies has successfully broken the world record for defrosting a car door.

While employed in 1960 as Third Secretary (Commercial) at the British Embassy in Vienna, he attended a fancy-dress party as Hamlet. This costume featured a borrowed satin blouse, a pair of brightly coloured tights and a wig. In one hand he clutched the skull of Yorick, which was represented by a Burmese tiger's skull into the cranium of which was set an ashtray and a receptacle for matches.

The party went with a swing and Mr Davies's attire was much acclaimed. Snow fell and, when he left, his Morris Minor was completely entombed. The Yorick skull had run out of matches and so he tried to unfreeze the lock with his breath. During this endeavour he became frozen to it and could only wave his Burmese tiger's skull to attract passers-by. He was found by two earnest Viennese policemen who hardly knew which aspect of the case to be alarmed by most.

The Least Successful Human Cannonball

In 1972 Miss Mary Connor made three fearless attempts to become the first woman ever to be blasted across the River Avon.

On the first occasion the cannon fired and nothing happened. On the second the cannon went off at half-cock and she swept gracefully into the air, getting at least halfway across the river.

However, her personal best came on the third attempt when she arrived, wearing a bandage round her ankle and plasters on both elbows, while explaining to bystanders that she had grazed them coming out of the cannon. She not only flew out this time and went into the river, back first, at exactly the same spot as before, but also capsized the rescue boat and had to swim to the bank.

This entirely surpasses the previous record, held by Miss Rita Thunderbird, who remained in the cannon while her bra shot across the River Thames.

The World Divorce Record Holder

On few men do the eternal bonds of holy matrimony have less of a grip than on Glynn de Moss 'Scotty' Wolfe. When we last heard of him he was just divorcing wife number 23 on the grounds that she used his toothbrush. By 1986 he had set a new world record of 26 divorces.

A former marriage guidance counsellor, he says, 'Everyone should get married. I always have been. Only the faces changed.'

Now eighty, he claims to remember the names of practically all his wives. 'Helen was first in 1931,' he said. 'Then came Marjorie, Margie, Mildred and Adele in quick succession. In 1943 I married Mary, but her father wanted to kill me and that put a damper on everything. Then there was Mary A., Peggy Lou, Beverley, Shirley, Sherri (twice), Kathy, Paulette, Didi, Bobbie, Demerle, Esther, Gloria, Maria, Lupitia Eva and then another Mary.'

Announcing that this could be true love at long last, he married Christine, wife number 26, in 1985. 'I feel good about this one,' Mr Wolfe said as he came out of the Las Vegas wedding chapel where the clerk in charge described the bride as 'a very nice lady except she had a lot of tattoos'.

Addressing reporters after the ceremony, Mr Wolfe said his only reservation about her was that 'she eats sunflower seeds in bed'. It lasted nine months.

He has paid more than $1 million in alimony and always keeps a couple of wedding dresses handy in the wardrobe. 'Divorce doesn't upset me,' he said. 'It's another raccoon skin on the wall.'

☞ 2 ☜

DOING IT AT WORK

The Least Successful Annual Conference
The Most Unsuccessful Inventor
The Least Successful Pier Demolition
The Worst Preacher
The Least Successful Animal Rescue
The Vet Who Surprised a Cow
The Worst Ship
The Least Successful Equal-Pay Advertisement
The Least Successful Experiment
The Slowest-Selling Postcard
The Least Successful Fire Station
The Least Successful Psychic Act
The Least Successful Bus Launch
The Worst Computer
The Most Unsuccessful Clairvoyants
The Least Successful Explorer
The Worst Magician
The Most Unsuccessful Lying-in-State

'Our business in life is not to succeed, but to continue to fail in good spirits.'
ROBERT LOUIS STEVENSON

The Least Successful Annual Conference

The British Association of Travel Agents held an outstanding annual conference at Sorrento in 1985. Delegates from Britain had already been doing solid work: the conference train was delayed by points failure at Purley; the flight was late; there was fog at Gatwick; most people arrived a day late; so many went down with food poisoning the ABTA doctor was singled out for special praise in the closing address; two fell down a marble staircase, and the marketing director of Kuoni Travel developed septicaemia following a snake bite.

Furthermore, organisers of the annual golf tournament arrived to find there wasn't a golf course in Sorrento so this popular event had to be held in Dublin.

However, it was Italian genius that brought this conference to a climax. Surrounded by marching bands and ceremonial guards, the Minister for Development addressed all the delegates in the forum at Pompeii. At this point a local travel agent, Lucio Aponte, decided this would be the ideal moment to fly overhead and drop 3,500 roses on the visitors.

The ceremony had just begun when a light aircraft appeared, swooped down, drowned out the Minister, dropped the roses and missed the forum completely. Minutes later it reappeared, flying even lower and causing the delegates to crouch. Five times he flew past and five times he missed the target. Not a single flower landed near the delegates, but there were roses all over Mount Vesuvius.

The Most Unsuccessful Inventor

Between 1962 and 1977 Mr Arthur Paul Pedrick patented 162 inventions, none of which was taken up commercially.

Among his greatest inventions were 'a bicycle with amphibious capacity', spectacles that improved vision in poor visibility, and an arrangement whereby a car might be driven from the back seat.

The grandest scheme of Mr Pedrick, who described himself as the 'One-Man-Think-Tank-Basic Physics Research Laboratory of 77 Hillfield Road, Selsey, Sussex', was to irrigate the deserts of the world by sending a constant supply of snowballs from the Polar regions through a network of giant pea-shooters.

He patented several golf inventions – including a golf ball that could be steered in flight – that contravened the rules of the game.

The Least Successful Pier Demolition

Margate Pier was declared dangerous in 1978 after violent gales lashed the Kent coast. It was thought best to pull the pier down before it collapsed.

In January 1979 a demolition team arrived and detonated an immense charge of gelignite. The explosion sent water hundreds of feet into the air, but left the pier's essential character unchanged. After a second 'demolition' a rivet was found embedded in the wall of a pub and police insisted that all future attempts should be made at high tide. The result was that explosion number four took place at midnight and woke up all Margate's seafront.

The demolition team made six further attempts before a Margate councillor suggested that, in view of the large crowds they drew, the unsuccessful explosions should be made a weekly tourist attraction.

After the fouteenth attempt, the demolition team was retired and a replacement company employed. After attempt number fifteen, the lifeboat house on the pier was seen to be at a slight angle.

The Worst Preacher

For sheer creative dullness the Revd Frederick Denison Maurice (1805–1872) has few equals. Of his sermons Mr Aubrey de Vere said, 'Listening to him was like eating pea soup with a fork.'

Like the members of his congregation, we shall never know what his sermons were about. Sir Mounstuart Grant was one of his most avid fans. 'I must have heard him, first and last, some thirty or forty times, and never carried away one clear idea, or even the impression that he had more than the faintest conception of what he himself meant.'

When asked to summarise a Maurice address, Dr Benjamin Jowett, Master of Balliol College, Oxford, replied, 'Well, all that I could make out was that today was yesterday and this world is the same as the next.'

The only serious competition comes from Dr Robert South who, in 1689, is said to have put his entire congregation to sleep, including the King of England.

At one point he interrupted his own sermon to say, 'My Lord Lauderdale, rouse yourself. You snore so loud that you will wake the King.'

The Least Successful Animal Rescue

The firemen's strike of 1978 made possible one of the great animal rescue attempts of all time. Valiantly, the British Army had taken over emergency fire-fighting and on 14 January they were called out by an elderly lady in south London to retrieve her cat, which had become trapped up a tree. They arrived with impressive haste and soon discharged their duty. So grateful was the lady that she invited them all in for tea. Driving off later, with fond farewells completed, they ran over the cat and killed it.

The Vet Who Surprised a Cow

In the course of his duties in August 1977, a Dutch veterinary surgeon was required to treat an ailing cow. To investigate its internal gases he inserted a tube into that end of the animal not capable of facial expression and struck a match. The jet flame set fire first to some bales of hay and then to the whole farm, causing damage estimated at £45,000. The vet was later fined £140 for starting a fire in a manner surprising to the magistrates. The cow escaped with shock.

The Worst Ship

Between 1953, when it was built, and 1976, when it sank, the *Argo Merchant* suffered every known form of maritime disaster.

In 1967 the ship took eight months to sail from Japan to America. It collided with a Japanese ship, caught fire three times and had to stop for repair on five occasions.

In 1968 there was a mutiny and in 1969 she went aground off Borneo for thirty-four hours. In the next five years she was laid up in Curaçao, grounded off Sicily and towed to New York.

In 1976 her boilers broke down six times and she once had to travel with two red lights displayed, indicating that the crew could no longer control the ship's movements because both the steering and the engine had failed. She was banned from Philadelphia, Boston and the Panama Canal.

To round off a perfect year she ran aground and sank off Cape Cod, depositing the country's largest oil slick on the doorstep of Massachusetts.

At the time of the final grounding the ship had been lost for over fifteen hours. The crew was eighteen miles off course and navigating by the stars, because their modern equipment had broken down. What is more, the West Indian helmsman could not read the Greek handwriting showing the course to be steered.

A naval expert afterwards described the ship as 'a disaster looking for somewhere to happen'.

The Least Successful Equal-Pay Advertisement

In 1976 the European Economic Community pointed out to the Irish government that it had not yet implemented the agreed sex-equality legislation. The Dublin government immediately advertised for an equal-pay enforcement officer. The advertisement offered different salary scales for men and women.

The Least Successful Experiment

A pioneering French inventor called Sauvant claimed in 1932 that he had perfected the world's first crash-proof aeroplane. From all accidents, he said, the aircraft and passengers would emerge completely unscathed.

On three occasions gendarmes removed the wheels from this contraption to prevent Monsieur Sauvant taking off in something that looked like a metallic boiled egg with prongs.

The irate inventor said it was perfectly safe and based on his own experiments showing that if a hen's egg is placed inside an ostrich egg the chicken embryo would be unaffected by the experience. As one French newspaper said, 'No explanation of how the smaller egg is placed inside the larger one has yet appeared, nor have we been told what fate befalls the ostrich.'

Eventually, Monsieur Sauvant persuaded several friends to push him off an eighty-foot cliff in Nice. Confident that they would see him step out triumphantly waving, they peered down at the beach to see wreckage shattered beyond all hope of reconstruction and an inventor too dazed to leave his vehicle without the assistance of ropes and a team of enthusiastic admirers.

Later, when he had recovered, he declared that he was delighted with the experiment.

The Slowest-Selling Postcard

The world's slowest-selling postcard depicts a fascinating fourteenth-century Tibetan rain bucket.

The inspired publications officer at the Victoria and Albert Museum had 5,000 copies of this exquisite card printed. Of these 24 were destroyed in a flood and 4,972 are still available. Only four were ever sold.

The Least Successful Fire Station

Roused by the alarm, the firemen of Arklow in County Wicklow raced to their posts in December 1984, only to find flames completely engulfing their own fire station. 'Christmas is always a busy time for us,' Mr Michael O'Neill, the Chief Fire Officer, said, explaining why the fire had raged unnoticed.

'The lads found their equipment and protective clothing had been destroyed and we watched the station burn to the ground,' he said philosophically. It was the second time Arklow fire station had burnt down in recent years.

The Least Successful Psychic Act

The hypnotist Romark announced in 1977 that he was going to give a public display of his psychic powers. 'I'm going to drive a car, blindfold, through Ilford,' he said.

On 12 October he duly placed two coins, a slice of dough and a thick band across his eyes. Shortly afterwards he climbed into a yellow Renault and set off down Cranbrook Road.

After twenty yards he drove confidently into the back of a parked police van. A large admiring crowd formed around our man who later said, 'That van was parked in a place that logic told me it wouldn't be.'

The Least Successful Bus Launch

With a great fanfare Bombardier (Ireland) Ltd launched 'the bus of the '80s'. The plan was to have the Irish Minister of Transport, Mr Reynolds, drive the first one out of the works on a triumphant tour of Limerick.

On 10 November 1980, he got into the bus but could not start it. Bombardier officials said the batteries were flat. New ones were fitted, but with no visible consequence. Technicians worked underneath the fine bus throughout the launching ceremony.

When the Minister threw the bottle of champagne he could not break it. Eventually, he hurled it with such violence that the Mayor of Limerick was drenched. 'It's all part of the risks attached to the office,' he said.

The Very Reverend Dean Emeritus M. J. Talbot prayed for the bus, whereupon the Minister drove out of the works hooting his horn en route to a reception at the Shamrock Hotel, Bunratty. Halfway there the bus broke down and the VIPs completed the journey by car.

In a speech applauding this excellent vehicle for the new age the Minister said that 'last week Mrs Reynolds and I launched a ship in Cork; there was not nearly as much excitement'.

The Worst Computer

It is widely suggested that computers improve efficiency. Lovers of vintage chaos might remember the computer installed in 1975 by Avon County Council to pay staff wages.

The computer's spree started off in a small way, paying a school caretaker £75 an hour instead of 75 pence. Then it got ambitious and did not pay a canteen worker at all for seven weeks.

Before long it got positively confident and paid a janitor £2,600 for a week's work. He sent the cheque back and received another for the same amount by return of post.

There was now no stopping it. A deputy headmistress received her year's annual salary once a month; heads of department earned less than their assistants, and some people had more tax deducted in a week than they earned all year.

In February 1976, 280 employees on the council payroll attended a protest meeting. Of these, only eight had been paid the correct salary. They all went on strike.

The Most Unsuccessful Clairvoyants

A convention of clairvoyants was held in April 1978 at the Sheraton Hotel in Paris. Readers of palms and tea-cups, tellers of tarot and gazers into crystal balls turned up in large numbers.

On the last day an English reporter asked if there would be another conference the next year. One of the clairvoyants replied, 'We don't know yet.'

The Least Successful Explorer

Thomas Nuttall (1786–1859) was a pioneer botanist whose main field of study was the flora of remote parts of north-west America. As an explorer, however, his work was characterised by the fact that he was almost permanently lost. During his expedition of 1812 his colleagues frequently had to light beacons in the evening to help him find his way back to the camp.

One night he completely failed to return and a search party was sent out. As it approached him in the darkness, Nuttall assumed they were Apaches and tried to escape. The annoyed rescuers pursued him for three days through bush and river until he accidentally wandered back into the camp.

On another occasion Nuttall was lost again and lay down exhausted. He looked so pathetic that a passing Apache, instead of scalping him, picked him up, carried him three miles to the river and paddled him home in a canoe.

The Worst Magician

It is quite possible that if Tommy Cooper's tricks had worked, no one would have heard of him. Happily, however, his magic was from the start blessed with an almost operatic badness. As a result he became a much loved household name.

It may be of interest to hear how this great man

discovered his unique gifts. At the age of seventeen, while an apprentice shipwright, he appeared in a public concert held at the firm's canteen at Hyde in Essex. Intending to give a serious display of magic, he walked onto the stage. As soon as the curtains parted, he forgot all his lines.

For a while he just stood there, opening his mouth only to close it again. The audience was spellbound. A star was born. 'All right,' he thought. 'Get on with it.'

He got on with it. Everything went wrong. His grand finale was a milk bottle trick. 'You have a bottle full of milk,' he told the entranced audience, 'and you put paper over the top. You turn the bottle upside-down, and take the paper away. The milk stays in.'

With bated breath, the audience watched. He turned the bottle. He paused for effect. He took away the paper. Drenched. All over him.

As if he had not done enough already, Mr Cooper then got stage fright and began moving his mouth furiously without any sound coming out. At this point he started to tremble and walked off, perspiring heavily.

Once in the wings, he heard the massed cheers of a standing ovation. His future glory was assured.

The Most Unsuccessful Lying-in-State

After their death bishops of many denominations are left lying about the church so that mourners may pay their last respects.

The most unsuccessful such event happened in March 1896 at a Greek Orthodox Church in Methymni.

After two days lying in state, clad in episcopal vestments, the Bishop of Lesbos, Nicephorus Glycas, suddenly sat bolt upright, glared at the mourners and asked, 'What are you staring at?'

3

MAKING THE MOST OF YOUR FREE TIME

The Worst Tourist
The Least Mysterious Mystery Tour
The Least Successful Balloon Flight
The Least Successful Attempt to Meet a Relative
at an Airport
The Worst Navigator
The Least Successful Attempt to Solve the Mystery
of the Loch Ness Monster
The Slowest Solution of a Crossword
The Least Successful Lion
The Least Comprehensible Camping Instructions
The Least Successful Birdwatching
The Most Chaotic Fishing Trip
The Least Successful Anglo-French Friendship Society
The Least Successful Historical Reconstruction
The Funeral that Disturbed the Corpse
The Least Successful Attempt to Clear Molehills
The Most Unsuccessful Angling Contest
The Least Successful Golf Club

'Tell me, Mr MacMahon, how long did it take you to learn to play chess so badly?'

'Sir, it's been nights of study and self-denial.'

CONVERSATION DURING A DISPLAY MATCH IN NORTHERN IRELAND IN 1947

The Worst Tourist

The least successful tourist on record is Mr Nicholas Scotti of San Francisco. In 1977 he flew from America to his native Italy to visit relatives.

En route the plane made a one-hour fuel stop at Kennedy Airport. Thinking that he had arrived, Mr Scotty got out and spent two days in New York believing he was in Rome.

When his nephews were not there to meet him, he assumed they had been delayed in the heavy Roman traffic mentioned in their letters. While tracking down their address, the great traveller could not help noticing that modernisation had brushed aside most, if not all, of the ancient city's landmarks.

He also noticed that many people spoke English with a distinct American accent. However, he just assumed that Americans got everywhere. Furthermore, he assumed it was for their benefit that so many street signs were written in English.

Mr Scotti spoke very little English himself and next asked the policeman (in Italian) the way to the bus depot. As chance would have it, the policeman came from Naples and replied fluently in the same tongue.

After twelve hours travelling round on a bus, the driver handed him over to a second policeman. There followed a brief argument in which Mr Scotti expressed amazement that the Rome police force would employ someone who did not speak his own country's language.

The great Scotti's brilliance is seen in the fact that even when told he was in New York, he refused to believe it.

To get him on a plane back to San Francisco, he was raced to the airport in a police car with sirens screaming. 'See,' said Scotti to his interpreter, 'I know I'm in Italy. That's how they drive.'

The Least Mysterious Mystery Tour

In 1971 Mr and Mrs William Farmer of Margate travelled to Wales for their summer holiday. At the start of the week they joined a British Rail mystery tour. It took them straight back to Margate. 'We were expecting the Welsh mountains,' they said afterwards.

'We nearly fell through the platform,' said Mr Farmer, who had been looking forward to getting away all summer. Declining a tour of the town, Mr and Mrs Farmer popped home for a cup of tea.

The Least Successful Balloon Flight

In 1823 Mr Charles Green, the pioneer balloonist, climbed into his basket and lit the take-off fire. The balloon rose slowly, but due to oversight or a practical joke the ropes were inadequately tied. The result was that the basket stayed behind on the ground. Rather than remain in it, Mr Green and a colleague clung onto the balloon hoop. Thus dangling, they floated over Cheltenham.

The Least Successful Attempt to Meet a Relative at an Airport

In 1975 Mrs Josephine Williams and her family went to meet a long-lost brother at Heathrow Airport. They took home a complete stranger.

Greatly relaxed by the in-flight drinking facilities, the traveller wandered into the airport lounge to be smothered by the kisses of Mrs Williams and her sisters. 'Gee, this is great,' he kept saying, all the while cuddling Mrs Williams in a manner she later described as 'not like a brother'.

His enthusiasm for British hospitality was modified, however, when Mr Williams shook his hand firmly and ushered him to a parked car.

They first suspected that something was amiss when their relative tried to jump out of the car while travelling at speed up the motorway.

When told that he was being taken to a family reunion in Coventry, he replied, 'Take my money. Here's my wallet. Take it and let me go.'

Slumped miserably in the front seat, he added, 'This is the first time I have been to England and I am being kidnapped.'

'I thought from the beginning he wasn't my brother,'

Mrs Williams said later, 'but my sisters wouldn't listen. They said I was only twelve when he left for America and wouldn't remember.'

The Worst Navigator

Mr Ronald Davies took over two years to make the voyage from Belfast to Plymouth. A less adventurous man would have done it in a few days. He left Ireland in 1974 because the UDA Protestants suspected him of working for the IRA while the IRA suspected him of working for British Intelligence. The situation was clearly impossible and so he set sail with his girlfriend, Brenda Collopy, aiming for the Isle of Man, in their seventeen-foot sloop, *Calcutta Princess*. In the months that followed they attracted six coastguard alerts, four lifeboat rescues and the assistance of a Royal Navy helicopter and the aircraft carrier *Hermes*.

On the first leg of their journey, to the Isle of Man, Mr Davies and Miss Collopy got lost and had to be guided into Douglas by a lifeboat. From there they went to Holyhead and set sail for Fishguard. When they failed to arrive, the coastguards mounted a search. The mariners eventually appeared in Waterford across the Irish Sea. They set course again for Fishguard, but turned up back in Holyhead. On the third attempt they made it to Fishguard.

Later, off the Devon coast, they had to be guided by radio into Clovelly. In Cornish waters their first port of call was Padstow, from where they set sail for Newquay. However, they were unable to find their way into the harbour and returned to Padstow, where they got caught in a storm and had to be rescued by the lifeboat.

At this point Miss Collopy left the boat and Mr Davies carried on alone. After a second rescue by the lifeboat from Padstow five weeks later, he made it as far as the waters of St Ives where, yet again, he had to be towed in by a life-boat. He completed the journey overland in August 1977.

The Least Successful Attempt to Solve the Mystery of the Loch Ness Monster

All attempts to find the Loch Ness monster failed. No one has failed more magnificently than four Hemel Hempstead firemen who in 1975 tried to seduce it.

Believing that feminine wiles would lure the beast from the deep, they built a thirty-foot-long papier-mâché female monster, equipped with long eyelashes, an outboard motor and a pre-recorded mating call. 'Sex solves everything,' said one of the firemen.

Painted blue and green, the monster then set off in search of romance with two firemen inside steering. They travelled fifteen miles offering flirtation and mystery, but encountered only sustained hormonal indifference from the deep. There are two possible reasons.

First, the firemen learned that their pre-recorded mating call was that of a bull walrus and so unlikely to interest the Ness beast.

Second, the outboard motor developed a fault during the voyage. The monster went into a flat spin, veered off backwards and crashed prostrate across a jetty.

No girl is at her best under these circumstances.

The Slowest Solution of a Crossword

On 4 April 1932 *The Times* of London printed its daily crossword.

In May 1966 the paper received a letter from a lady in Fiji announcing that she had just completed it. Apparently her mother had started it, but tasted defeat over clues like 'Islanders who end in rebellion' (eight letters).

The newspaper then lined a trunk for some years, which was the only sensible way to pass the Second World War. It was next found in an English attic by the lady in Fiji's sister who regularly posted crosswords to her puzzle-mad relative.

Over the years she worried away at it . . . until an 'S' appeared on the end of the rebellious islanders. An initial 'C' followed and a tell-tale 'P' became the third letter: 'Cypriots'. Thirty-four years will be extremely difficult to beat.

The Least Successful Lion

In 1970 a lion escaped from a circus in Italy. Typically, it found a small boy and started to chase him.

Less typically the small boy's mother turned on the lion and badly mauled it. The animals suffered severe head and skin wounds, and received treatment for shock.

The Least Comprehensible Camping Instructions

Few campsites are blessed with such comprehensive regulations as Camping Atlanta at Lungomare Sud in Italy.

After the general instruction that 'cars must enter or go away from the camp with motors out' we reach the all-embracing rule 15, which reads:

then is strictly forbidden to:
a) Reserve box parking, spaces with chairs, fences, rape or other means
b) Dainage of the plants and equiman
c) Not teak paper other box
d) Dig simples around tents
e) Play with ball of tamboury in the camp
f) Set to go into the camp, not authorised from the direction

So that campers know exactly where they stand, rule 17 concludes: 'The above listed rules are inappellable. All of the camping personnel are authorised to send away anyone who does follow them.'

The Least Successful Birdwatching

In November 1989 two hundred birdwatchers from all over Britain gathered in the Scilly Isles to see the arrival of an extremely rare grey-cheeked thrush. During the long wait they discussed the bird's North African habitat, its delicate colouring and the precise intonation of its unusually melodious call.

Peering through binoculars, they saw the priceless bird fly in amid exclamations regarding its beauty. As soon as it landed on the campsite at St Mary's Garrison, Mrs S. Burrow's cat, Muffin, dashed out, snatched the thrush in its mouth, disappeared into a bush and brought the birdwatching session to a close.

The Most Chaotic Fishing Trip

It was the perfect day for fishing. Leaving his farm on the North Kent coast one bright Thursday in August 1981, Mr John Jenkins took his family to the nearby resort of Seasalter.

Three-quarters of a mile out onto the mudflats his four-wheel-drive Dodge got stuck. Mr Jenkins made the long trek back to a telephone and called out one of his tractors. As soon as it arrived, this got stuck as well. The family climbed out and watched as the tide covered both vehicles.

On the Friday morning the first tractor was pulled out by a second. Together they set off to rescue the

Dodge, but en route both got stuck and were engulfed by the incoming tide.

Mr Jenkins now had three vehicles under water and so set out with his third tractor to remedy the situation. In rescuing the Dodge car this tractor also became stuck and that night it too disappeared beneath the waves.

By Saturday morning word had spread of this great sea adventure and whole families travelled out across the mud to watch a mechanical digger arrive and release one tractor before itself becoming wedged in the mud. By Saturday night that was under water as well.

On Sunday morning the rescued tractor went back to assist, whereupon it became immediately stuck in the mud and the tide covered the entire contents of Mr Jenkins's garage.

The Least Successful Anglo-French Friendship Society

Cross-Channel confusion reached new heights in 1985 after the inspired twinning of Godalming in Surrey with Joigny in France, two towns notable for having nothing whatever in common.

Relations got off to a cracking start at the twinning ceremony. Perhaps wishing to show a Gallic side to his nature, the English President, Sir Richard Posnett, greeted the French visitors with a fine speech in which he said, 'I kiss all your women.' Unknown to him, the word *baiser* has acquired earthy four-letter overtones since his schooldays and the French were appalled to hear that Sir Richard was intending to fornicate with everybody.

Joigny wanted to send their many children on exchange schemes, but Godalming had an older population and could muster only nine infants. Instead they were keen to send over the Godalming Amateur Dramatic Society to perform an evening of old-time music-hall. Overwhelming reluctance greeted this entire prospect in France, where a bicycle race round Godalming was suggested.

In Surrey this was felt likely to clog up the roads and so they proposed a swimming contest, but La Société de Natation de Joigny said the swimmers should meet for a banquet first, an idea the British resisted. The French then sent over the Joigny Chorale ('une très, très bonne chorale'). In Godalming they assumed it was a religious choir and booked the chapel at Charterhouse School only to find that it was 'a chaotic rock group who spent most of their time talking to each other between numbers'.

Things came to a head in 1987 when the Godalming Amateur Dramatic Society decided to hire a venue in Joigny and put on their old-time music-hall without waiting to be invited. The French accused 'Sir Posnett' of inflicting this entertainment on them and they then resigned from the friendship circle *en masse* as a protest against the British.

In recognition of this great achievement Joigny was, that very week, awarded Le Drapeau d'Amitié Européenne, the EEC's highest award for spreading European friendship.

The Least Successful Historical Reconstruction

The Battle of Waterloo in 1815 began when the Highland Regiment marched through the town at 4 a.m. playing bagpipes.

When the Napoleonic Association attempted an accurate reconstruction in 1985 at the site of the original battle, the local Waterloo council would allow only one piper to play at 4 a.m., providing he marched through the back streets. Drowsy residents thought it was a cat being strangled.

Neither side camped on the battlefield. The French army stayed at a girls' school and the British were put up in a mental institution from which the inmates had been evicted for the weekend.

The Belgian participants were so obsessed with ceremonial marching that everyone was exhausted by the time the battle started. Then three Napoleons turned up, which confused everyone. Furthermore, Wellington was not allowed to take his sword on the British Airways flight and so entered the fray unarmed. There was only one cannon and this had to leave halfway through the battle in order to arrive at Dunkirk in time for the ferry home. The British were outnumbered eight to one because everybody preferred the French uniforms and the final result was unclear.

When they finally got back onto British soil their only welcome was from HM Customs who confiscated their cannon for three hours.

The Funeral That Disturbed the Corpse

Perhaps the most unsuccessful funeral ever held was that of a Christian missionary called Schwartz. The service was held in Delhi at the end of the last century and culminated in the congregation singing the favourite hymn of the recently deceased Dr Schwartz. The mourners were surprised during the final verse to hear a voice from the coffin joining in.

The Least Successful Attempt to Clear Molehills

Tired of the ten large molehills that flourished on his lawn, Mr Oscar Ejiamike decided to remove them. After a vigorous campaign of bombing, gassing and waiting around in the dark with a raised shovel he found that the ten molehills survived intact. There were also twenty-two new ones.

At this point our man decided to 'surprise the moles' with a midnight poisoning raid. In May 1984 he drove his Jaguar 2.4 Automatic to the edge of the lawn and trained the headlamps on the enemy zone. While reaching across for the poison, Mr Ejiamike knocked the car into reverse and accelerated through the wall of his cottage, knocking over the electric heater, bursting his petrol tank, setting fire to his newly decorated sitting room and wrecking his car.

While this certainly surprised the moles, it had no effect on the thirty-two molehills. Next morning Mr Ejiamike bought twenty-two bags of ready-mixed cement and announced that he was going to concrete the lawn over.

The Most Unsuccessful Angling Contest

This fine event occurred during the National Ambulance Servicemen's Angling Championship held at Kidderminster in 1972.

Two hundred ambulance men gathered along the nearby canal and took part in five hours of keenly competitive fishing. In this time not one of them caught a single fish.

They would still be there now had not a passer-by – after watching them for some minutes – informed them that all the fish had been moved to other waters three weeks before.

The Least Successful Golf Club

The City Golf Club in London is unique among such organisations in not possessing a golf course, ball, tee, caddy or bag. In its entire premises just off Fleet

Street there is not a single photograph of anything that approaches a golfing topic.

'We had a driving range once,' the commissionaire said, 'but we dropped that years ago.' The membership now devotes itself exclusively to eating and drinking, which is much more sensible.

4

THE IMPORTANCE OF INDIVIDUALISM

The Most Pointless Petition
The Worst Phrasebook
The Noisiest Burglar
The Least Successful Attempt to Light a Coal Fire
The Least Effective Deaf Aid
The Worst Voyage
The Worst Driver (Male)
The Worst Driver (Female)
The Least Successful Round-the-World Cyclist
The Least Successful Football Trainer
The Woman Who Couldn't Organise a Piss-up
in a Brewery
The Least Successful Attempt to Raise
Money for Charity
The Least Successful Do-It-Yourself Expert
The Worst Cough
The Least Successful Attempt to Tranquillise
an Animal
The Least Successful Gas Conversion
The Most Noticeable Burglar

'Every man has a scheme that will not work.'

HOWE'S LAW

The Most Pointless Petition

In this genre the great A. N. Wilson is unsurpassed. During the autumn of 1987 the contemporary novelist became enraged that Poets' Corner in Westminster Abbey had no memorial bust honouring Matthew Arnold.

With a faultless display of campaigning skills, he fired off letters pointing out this disgraceful neglect and organised a petition of right-thinking literati, headed by the biographer Victoria Glendinning and Auberon Waugh, the editor of the *Literary Review*.

In a crusading editorial Mr Waugh wrote that 'unlike many of those whose monuments adorn the Abbey, Arnold's reputation has stood the test of time, and continued exclusion seems shameful'. He urged his readers to write immediately to the Right Reverend Dean of Westminster, who was instantly submerged in a barrage of irate mail.

This campaign reached the perfect conclusion when the Dean wrote back thanking them for their interest and pointing out that their proposals seemed to overlook the extremely lifelike bust of Arnold which had been in the Abbey since 1891.

The Worst Phrasebook

Pedro Carolino is one of the all-time greats. In 1883 he wrote an English–Portuguese phrasebook despite having little or no command of the English language.

His greatly recommended book, *The New Guide of the Conversation in Portuguese and English*, has now been reprinted under the title *English As She Is Spoke*.

After a brief dedication:

> We expect then, who the little book 'for the care what we wrote him, and for her typographical correction) that may be worth the acceptation of the studious persons, and especially of the youth, at which we dedicate him particularly.

Carolino kicks off with some 'Familiar Phrases' that the Portuguese holidaymaker might find useful. Among these are:

> Dress your hairs.
> This hat go well.
> Undress you to.
> Exculpate me by your brother's.
> She make the prude.
> Do you cut the hairs?
> He has tost his all good.

He then moves on to 'Familiar Dialogues', which included 'For to wish the good morning', and 'For to visit a sick'.

Dialogue 18 – 'For to ride a horse' – begins: 'Here is a horse who have bad looks. Give me another. I will

not that. He not sall know to march, he is pursy, he is
foundered. Don't you are ashamed to give me a jade as
like? he is unshoed. he is with nails up.' In the section on
'Anecdotes' Carolino offers the following humorous tale,
which is guaranteed to enthral any listener:

> One-eyed was laied against a man which had good eyes
> that he saw better than him. The party was accepted. I
> had gain, over said the one-eyed; why I se you two eyes,
> and you not look me who one.

It is difficult to top that, but Carolino manages in a useful section of 'Idiotisms and Proverbs'. These include:

> Nothing some money, nothing of Swiss.
> He eat to coaches.
> A take is better than two you shall have.
> The stone as roll not heap up not foam.

There is also the well-known expression: The dog that
bark not bite.

Carolino's particular genius was aided by the fact
that he did not possess an English–Portuguese diction-
ary. What he did possess were Portuguese–French and
French–English dictionaries through both of which he
dragged his original expressions. The results yield language of originality and great beauty. Is there anything
in conventional English that could equal the vividness
of 'To craunch a marmoset'?

The Noisiest Burglar

A Parisian burglar set new standards for the entire criminal world when, on 4 November 1933, he attempted to rob the home of an antique dealer. In the interests of disguise he was dressed in a fifteenth-century suit of armour, which dramatically limited his chances of both success and escape. He had not been in the house many minutes before its owner was awakened by the sound of clanking metal.

The owner got up and went out onto the landing where he saw the suit of armour climbing the stairs. He straightaway knocked the burglar off balance, dropped a small sideboard across his breastplate and went off to call the police.

Under cross-examination a voice inside the armour confessed to being a thief trying to pull off a daring robbery. Unfortunately for our man, the pressure of the sideboard had so dented his breastplate that it was impossible to remove the armour for twenty-four hours, during which period he had to be fed through the visor.

The Least Successful Attempt to Light a Coal Fire

In 1972, Derek Langborne, a scientist from Upton, near Didcot, built a fire in his grate and lit it. He then popped outside to fill the coal scuttle.

When he returned, he observed that, in its enthusiasm to heat the room, one log had rolled out of the grate and set fire to the log box. He picked it up and carried it out into the garden. On the way out he brushed against a curtain covering the front door. By the time he returned, the curtain and the door were both in flames.

While dialling the number for Didcot Fire Brigade, he noticed that the log box, which he had deposited in the garden, had now set fire to his car.

He then put on his overcoat and approached the car with a bucket of water. In the process he tripped over a partly filled petrol can.

Seeing that Mr Langborne was on good form, his neighbour called the fire brigade. By the time they arrived, Mr Langborne was himself was on fire with flames now leaping freely from his overcoat.

The Least Effective Deaf Aid

During a visit to his doctor in March 1978, Mr Harold Senby of Leeds found that his hearing improved when the aid he had been wearing for the past twenty years was removed. 'With it in I couldn't hear much,' he said. 'But with it out I had almost perfect hearing.'

Closer medical examination revealed that in the 1950s a deaf-aid mould was made for his left ear instead of his right. 'Over the years I have been fitted with several new aids, but no one noticed that I had been wearing them in the wrong hole.'

The Worst Voyage

Mr William Smith of Norfolk sailed from Scotland to Great Yarmouth in August 1978. Showing great independence of mind en route, he missed Bridlington harbour by four hundred yards and rammed a jetty; at Yarmouth he overshot by ninety miles and later ran aground off Kent.

A full-scale search for the boat was hampered by the change in its appearance. When it left Scotland, it was black with one mast. When rescued, it had two masts and was painted green. 'I passed the time while I was aground redecorating,' Mr Smith explained.

Entering Yarmouth harbour, he scraped a floating museum, collided with a small coaster and hit an entrant for the Tall Ships yacht race. He also knocked several guard rails of a trimaran and got the ropes of the cargo vessel *Grippen* wrapped round his mast.

Describing the voyage as 'pleasant with no hassles or worries', Mr Smith said he planned sailing to Australia next.

The Worst Driver (Male)

The world record for the most traffic offences in the shortest period of time is held by a man from Frisco in Texas, who achieved this feat in the first twenty minutes of car ownership.

Having hitch-hiked to the nearby city of McKinney

on 15 October 1966, he bought a 1953 Ford and drove out of the used-car showroom at 3.50 p.m.

At 3.54 he collided with a 1952 Chevrolet driven by a local woman, Mrs Wilma Smith Bailey, at the corner of McKinney and Heard Street.

One minute later he collided again, ninety feet south of Virginia Street and Tennessee Street, with another Chevrolet driven by Mrs Sally Whitsel of Farmersville.

Feeling more confident now in his new vehicle, he next drove around the courthouse one-way system in the wrong direction. Forty-six feet later he hit a 1963 Ford. It was still only 3.58.

He continued in this vein until 4.15 p.m. when he was in deep conversation with Patrolman Richard Buchan an, having just hit a Ford Mustang in Louisiana Street.

In the space of just twenty minutes he had acquired ten traffic tickets, caused six accidents, hit four cars without stopping and driven on the wrong side of the road four times.

When questioned, this determined motorist, who had not driven for ten years, said, 'They don't drive like they used to.'

The Worst Driver (Female)

Few motorists have shown quite so much natural confidence on the road as Miss Bessie Cash, who graced Oldham with her skills until 1982 when she voluntarily handed in her driving licence for her own safety.

After forty years with a clean motoring record Miss Cash suddenly pulled that something extra out of the bag. Although travelling a customary route to her home address in Orange Avenue, she suddenly took the wrong turning and went down a cul-de-sac, onto the pavement, past thirteen shop fronts, down a subway, through a labyrinth of tunnels, up into a shopping precinct, down another subway, in and out of some trees, narrowly missing forty-three shoppers and Miss Eunice Gerrard, a traffic warden, up onto another pavement, in and out of some more trees and straight at a policeman, who tried to stop her, but had to jump out of the way and then watched her drive past a 'No Entry' sign and right into a police panda car. This brought her to the road she had been looking for.

Of Miss Cash's driving, Miss Gerrard, the traffic warden, said, 'I saw a green mini going down the subway. I thought, "No, it can't be." I ended up chasing it in and out of the trees.'

Explaining the incident, Miss Cash said afterwards, 'I just lost my way.' Realising that she could not improve on this performance, she retired at her peak and has not driven again.

The Least Successful Round-the-World Cyclist

Mr Michael Murphy, a twenty-two-year-old draughtsman from Stevenage in Hertfordshire, set off in August

1975 to cycle round the world. During the next two years he was robbed by Yugoslavian peasants, stoned by tribesmen in the Khyber Pass and nearly froze to death in a blizzard.

When he finally arrived back in England in April 1977, he had only to collect his bike at Heathrow Airport and cycle the last forty miles home. After 25,000 miles he confidently expected to make it back to Stevenage. His hopes were crushed, as was his bicycle, by a conveyor belt joining the plane to the customs hall. He had to hitch a lift home.

The Least Successful Football Trainer

In the first ever World Cup the trainer of the American soccer team set an example that no other has yet managed to equal. In the 1930s semi-final Argentina had just scored a disputed goal against the USA. Shouting abuse at the referee as he travelled, our fellow dashed out to tend an injured player.

The 80,000 crowd roared with approval as he ran onto the pitch, threw down his medical bag, broke a bottle of chloroform and anaesthetised himself. He was carried off by his own team.

The Woman Who Couldn't Organise a Piss-up in a Brewery

In the 1970s a woman reporter, working for the *Daily*

Mirror, was chided by her colleagues that 'she couldn't organise a piss-up in a brewery'. Piqued by this comment, she announced that the following week contained her birthday and she would be arranging a party at the Fullers Brewery in Chiswick.

With a touch of sheer brilliance, she put the wrong day on the notice board and revellers turned up twenty-four hours early.

The Least Successful Attempt to Raise Money for Charity

In 1986 Mr Jeffrey Gill decided to raise £1,000 for the Bude coastguards by windsurfing from the North Devon coast to Lundy Island.

When, several hours later, there was no sign of him, the coastguards launched a full-scale air-sea rescue operation involving the Bristol Channel lifeboat, the Lundy ferry, the Bude inflatable life-raft, a helicopter from RAF Chivenor and mobile coastguard units from as far away as Cornwall. The total cost of the operation was £2,000, exactly twice what he had hoped to raise.

Eventually, he was found, substantially becalmed and floating towards America. 'The wind dropped and my flares didn't work,' said Mr Gill, who runs a shop in Widemouth Bay called Outdoor Adventure.

The Least Successful Do-It-Yourself Expert

An ever popular field, DIY has produced an astonishing crop of cult figures. Supreme in this category is Mr Anthony Drew of Kent who showed the way with his imaginative attempt to renew a shower curtain.

Sensing the untold possibilities of a ladder, he managed in a single manoeuvre to fall off and splinter the bath enamel, while his hammer cracked the bath and his drills smashed the basin. Resting briefly, he went downstairs to repair the fireplace and poked his hammer through the TV screen before returning to his real favourite, the ladder.

Moving outside, he climbed it once more to paint the bathroom window. With grown-up consistency he fell off again. This time his chisel flew through the window and cracked the lavatory bowl, while Mr Drew himself went hurtling through the roof of his carport.

But for sheer elegant simplicity no one can beat Michael Taylor of Gloucester, who decided to lower the floor of his cellar and make it an extra room. He dug away the foundations and the entire building collapsed.

The Worst Cough

In 1988 Alan Parkes of Sydney had what is widely thought to be the most troublesome cough in modern history. His constant hacking in the middle of the night terrified the woman next door who woke up and thought it was gunfire. Assuming there was a crazed gunman on the loose, she barricaded herself into her bedroom and called the police.

Minutes later armed officers poured in from all over Sydney, including members of a crack 'tactical response group'. Within half an hour they had surrounded Alan's house and taken up siege positions in readiness for a shoot-out.

With marksmen crouching right round the suburb, their leader knocked on the door. When it opened and our man stood there choking in winter-weight pyjamas, neither party could believe what they were seeing. Mr Parkes, who is a council-tip worker, promised to get some lozenges.

The Least Successful Attempt to Tranquillise an Animal

Mr Donald Kelly made his contribution to the art of tranquillisation at Salem, Vancouver, in July 1980. While he was attempting to sedate an over-exuberant donkey, the syringe filled with Rompun, a horse tranquilliser, slipped.

He put out his hand to catch it, but the needle went into his ring finger. During the sleep which followed, Mr Kelly, an animal control officer, was described as 'looking very peaceful'. The donkey continued with its plans for the rest of the evening.

The Least Successful Gas Conversion

Since converting his orange Volvo to gas power for reasons of economy, Mr Tony Forward proudly said he had enjoyed two years of trouble-free motoring. In that time he had only once experienced any kind of bother with it.

In the early hours of the morning in 1981 there was a loud explosion, which had woken not only him but also the entire population of Derby Green, a small hamlet in Hampshire. Thinking it might be a thunderbolt, he went outside to find that the blast from his car had destroyed his garage and conservatory, scattered his freezer and its contents over the garden, blown a hole in his neighbours' garage, damaging their car, and left the fence and his own personally modified Volvo in flames. Such was the heat that a spare gas cylinder on the back seat went up and sent the roof of his car flying through the air and crashing through trees into a garden across the road.

Apart from this one incident Mr Forward experienced no trouble at all.

The Most Noticeable Burglar

Very few house-breakers give genuine pleasure and entertainment. In February 1981 a young Soviet burglar broke into a flat at Baku on the Caspian Sea, while the owners were away on holiday. Exhausted by all the looting, he ran himself a soothing hot bath and then sat down to pour himself a couple of vodkas. Feeling peckish, he knocked up a little something to eat.

Thoroughly relaxed, he poured more vodka, strolled over to the upright piano and started playing Grieg's Piano Concerto. After the resounding C major *sforzando* chord he was just starting the *animato* section and bursting into song (although strictly speaking no words were actually written for the piece) when the police arrived, alerted by the complaints of several philistine neighbours.

5

THE BUSINESS OF POLITICS

The Least Charismatic Politician
The Least Appropriate Speech
The Most Pointless By-Election
The Worst Mayor
The Least Successful Politicians
The Worst Speech Writer
The Least Eloquent Lords
The Least Successful Protest March
The Politician Who Did Not Have a Motion Seconded
in His Entire Career
The Most Failed Assassination Attempts on a
Political Leader
The Worst Hijackers
The Least Successful National Mourning
The Least Successful Terrorists
The Least Successful Coup

'Politics is a field where the choice lies between two blunders.'

JOHN MORLEY MP, FEBRUARY 1887

'Well, thank God, at last we have got a ministry without one of those men of genius in it.'

A PEER COMMENTING ON LORD ADDINGTON'S NEWLY FORMED GOVERNMENT, 1801

The Least Charismatic Politician

In one of the outstanding political campaigns of the twentieth century Mrs Beryl Shakes announced that she would be standing for Parliament on condition that she did not have to speak in public, attend meetings, talk to journalists or visit the constituency. 'Beryl's a shy person and she hasn't done anything like this before,' Mrs Mary Sanders, her party agent, said.

When selected as the Democratic Party candidate for Napier at Hawke's Bay in the 1987 New Zealand general election, Mrs Shakes said, 'I won't go to Hawke's Bay. I want to stay at home and support my husband.' (Mr Graham Shakes was standing as the Democratic candidate for Wairarapa.)

A local newspaper profile of this exciting candidate said that she 'was educated at Wellington Technical College and took up sewing before her marriage'. She is also 'a keen gardener and a member of the Wairarapa branch of the New Zealand Soil Association'.

According to Norm Daken, who covered the campaign for the local *Hawke's Bay Herald Tribune*, 'We believe Mrs Shakes did visit the constituency for one day as part of her campaign, but we were not told of that event and had no opportunity to see her.'

When the votes were counted, she polled a magnificent

534, while her husband, who had campaigned enthusiastically throughout, got 27 amid cries of 'Good one, Graham.'

The Least Appropriate Speech

There have been few more fearless exponents of free speech than Baroness Trumpington of Sandwich. On 14 July 1986 she gave a powerful address to the House of Lords in the British Parliament on the subject of 'expenses paid to childminders'.

'There has been much confusion on this matter,' she declaimed, her splendid sentiments resounding across that ancient chamber. Their lordships listened in respectful silence and she called for a sane and sensible approach.

She had spoken for five minutes when this free-ranging diatribe built to an impressive climax. 'My lords,' she said, 'I have been speaking on the wrong subject.'

The debate was, in fact, on an amendment to the Social Security Bill. Tragically, she could have spoken for much longer, as not all of their lordships had noticed. Giving away a trick of the trade, the Baroness said that she had brought the wrong notes.

The Most Pointless By-Election

We are still waiting for the definitive by-election at which no candidates poll any votes at all. But the great Gatting contest of 1816 comes close.

The constituency only had three voters: Sir Mark Wood, his son (who had gone missing) and their butler, Jennings. All was peaceful and Sir Mark nominated his son as the Tory candidate. The butler refused to second him after a row with his boss and in a fit of pique revealed his own intention to stand, whereupon Sir Mark refused to second him.

We were approaching the perfect by-election with no votes or candidates when everyone seconded everyone else and the result was:

Mark Wood junior (Tory) (absent) 1
Jennings (Whig) 0

It was the only election ever held in this promising constituency. Gatting was disenfranchised in 1832. The loss to British politics is incalculable.

The Worst Mayor

From our point of view the most important mayor ever to hold office was Señor Jose Ramon Del Cuet.

In June 1978 he resigned as Mayor of Coacaloco in Mexico, announcing that his record in office was poor. This selfless decision was reached with the help of four thousand local voters who stormed the town hall, seized the mayor and forced him to eat twelve pounds of bananas before signing his resignation.

The Least Successful Politicians

Only eight politicians have been awarded the ultimate accolade by the British electorate. The pioneer was Lord Garvagh. When standing as Liberal candidate for Reigate in 1832, he evoked such widespread indifference that he became the first person to poll no votes at all in a general election.

The excitement was intense. It was not until seven years later that Mr L. Oliphant (Liberal) was able to repeat the achievement.

In 1841 two Chartists, Mr W. Thomason and Mr W. Edwards, did it at Paisley and Monmouth respectively. Six years later a third Chartist, Mr G. T. Harney, repeated the triumph at Tiverton and before long the Chartists were out of business altogether.

Representing the Conservative Party, Viscount Lascelles threw caution to the wind in 1847. He made the breakthrough at Tewkesbury where it proved so popular that Mr H. Brown repeated the feat on behalf of the Liberal Party in 1859.

The last person to achieve nought was Mr F. R. Lees at the 1860 Ripon by-election. The art has been completely lost since candidates are now allowed to vote for themselves.

The Worst Speech Writer

Warren Gamaliel Harding wrote all his own speeches

when President of the USA in the 1920s and people queued up to pay tribute.

H. L. Mencken said, 'He writes the worst English that I have ever encountered. It is so bad that a sort of grandeur creeps into it.'

When Harding died, e. e. cummings said, 'The only man, woman or child who wrote a simple declarative sentence with seven grammatical errors is dead.'

Here is a rewarding sample of the man's style: 'I would like the government to do all it can to mitigate, then, in understanding, in mutuality of interest, in concern for the common good, our tasks will be solved.'

The Least Eloquent Lords

Richard Coke, the fifth Earl of Leicester, was a member of the House of Lords for twenty-two years before making his only speech. In so doing he ended an illustrious family record for complete silence. His father did not speak in thirty-two years of membership; nor his grandfather in sixty-seven. This meant that no Coke spoke for a hundred and twenty years.

The third Earl once shouted 'jolly good' during somebody else's speech, but then you have to wait until the early 1960s for anything comparable (the fifth Earl said he would like to speak on capital punishment, but then changed his mind).

Richard Coke explained that they were all too busy running a sub-post office at their stately home, Holkham

Hall in Norfolk, which the first Earl had opened in 1834.

Then, in January 1972, the fifth Earl decided that he would 'rather like to take the plunge'. He started with a joke. 'This is not a case of too many Cokes spoiling the broth,' he said.

He went on to say that pollution was a bad thing and that untested artificial fertilisers were ruining the countryside.

'It took a lot out of me,' said the Earl, whose family motto is 'He is prudent who is patient.'

The Least Successful Protest March

On 26 May 1979 the British Communist Party organised a day trip to Calais for a protest march against the Common Market. There was to have been a mass march through the streets, led by a jazz band and a reception with Monsieur Jean-Jacques Barthes, the Communist mayor.

When the 250 British day-trippers arrived at Calais harbour, they heard that the march had been called off because of the rain. They were also told that the jazz band would not be arriving. 'They were too expensive,' a tour operator said at the docks, 'and they wanted to bring a piano.'

In any case, it was discovered that the British had left their banner in the coach at Dover and the French would not know what they were demonstrating about. In spite of this, the visitors decided to hold a short march from the lunch to the meeting hall. However, the lunch venue was changed at the last minute and the hall turned out to be across the road. 'It's not really far enough to march,' commented their director, Mr Landen Temple.

After the speeches Mr Temple announced that the mayoral reception was off. Apparently the room had been double-booked with a convention of football referees who took precedence.

Furthermore, an international meeting of trade unionists planned for four o'clock had been mistakenly held while the British delegation was having lunch. Also, the social evening with the Calais Young Communists was cancelled because they turned out to be a serious bunch who wanted to have a meeting instead.

'It's been a bit of a mess all round,' said Mr Temple with an engaging smile.

The Politician Who Did Not Have a Motion Seconded in His Entire Career

In sixteen years on Huddersfield Council, Alderman William Wheatley never had a motion seconded.

Between 1905 and 1921 this excellent man, a member of the Labour Party, regularly put motions before the Council on a wide range of topics. Not once in that period was any member of the Council sufficiently keen on his suggestion to vote that it even be discussed.

A Wheatley relative said, 'In our family we have a saying: "You're as useless as Uncle William."'

The Most Failed Assassination Attempts on a Political Leader

By 1974 an estimated twenty-four attempts had been made on Fidel Castro's life by political enemies. By 1978 the estimate of sixty was mentioned by Castro himself.

One plot failed because two poison capsules dissolved while hidden in a pot of cold cream. Another came unstuck because the brunette agent sent to finish Castro off turned out to be in love with him.

Badly aimed poison pellets did more damage to Cuban trees than to the country's leader and, according to one story, an array of exploding seashells missed Castro by forty minutes, but fused all the traffic lights in downtown Havana.

Three assassins were arrested carrying a bazooka across a university campus and another put a poisoned chocolate milkshake in the freezer compartment by mistake. By the time anyone offered this to Castro, it had gone solid and was impossible to drink.

The Worst Hijackers

We shall never know the identity of the man who in 1976 made the most unsuccessful hijack attempt ever. On the flight across America he rose from his seat and took the stewardess hostage.

'Take me to Detroit,' he said.

'We are already going to Detroit,' she replied.

'Oh . . . good,' he said, and sat down again.

The Least Successful National Mourning

India was swept with grief on 22 March 1979 when the Indian Prime Minister, Mr Morarji Desai, informed Parliament that Jayaprakash Narayan, the patriot and elder statesman, had died in a Bombay Hospital.

The Prime Minister delivered a moving eulogy and Parliament was adjourned. Flags were lowered to half-mast.

The news flashed all over the subcontinent. Funereal music was broadcast on All-India Radio. Schools and shops closed down throughout the land. The entire nation was plunged into mourning for over an hour.

Everyone was shaken by the news, none more so than Mr Jayaprakash Narayan, who was in bed convalescing.

'I'm sorry about that,' said the Prime Minister afterwards. The information had apparently come from the Director of the Intelligence Bureau, one of whose staff had seen a body being carried out of the hospital.

The Least Successful Terrorists

Few urban guerrillas have inspired less fear or wreaked less havoc than the Gatti Gang, who were the outstanding terrorists of their generation. A Milan-based cell of Italy's Red Brigade, they only ever had one bomb and were so scared of it that a fellow terrorist told them to 'give up. You're a danger to everyone.'

Most of their robbery plans had to be shelved because none of them could drive a car. They had to travel everywhere by bus and one bank raid was carried out on a motor scooter. When they did stage a hold-up to raise funds for their subversive activities, they got away with 18,000 lire (£9).

All their pistols were too rusty to fire and, while trying to replace them, they were swindled out of £1,000 in an arms deal that went wrong. The group's strategy meetings often had to be postponed because the leader, Enrico Gatti, was nearly always suffering from a heavy cold.

The gang's finest hour came when Senor Gatti gave himself up and urged the other twenty-seven to throw in the towel. 'Desert,' he told a packed courtroom. 'It's all over. Ten years of struggle have brought us nothing but tears. Lots of our young members want to go home and live in peace.'

The Least Successful Coup

In 1964 in a Fascist coup was organised in Rome. Gathering on the outskirts of the city, the right-wingers planned a stampede to the centre prior to over throwing the government.

However, the majority were not from Rome itself and so the stampede got lost in the back streets.

Five years after the coup, the authorities discovered that this had taken place and set up a commission to investigate it.

6

WAR AND PEACE

The Soldier Who Caused Most Chaos
The Worst Submarine
The Least Successful Air Attack
The Worst General
The Fastest Defeat in a War
The Soldiers Who Fought the Second World War
Longest
The Country That Fought Two World Wars
Simultaneously
The Least Successful Torpedo
The Least Successful Weapons
The Least Successful Target Practice
The Worst Tactician
The Worst Arms Expert
The Most Unsuccessful Nine-Gun Salute
The Worst Ever Duel
The Least Bellicose War
The Least Successful Undercover Operation
The Least Successful Manoeuvre
The Least Successful Attempt to Opt Out

'C'est magnifique mais ce n'est pas la guerre.'
MARSHAL PIERRE BOSQUET

The Soldier Who Caused Most Chaos

In the military world Dan Raschen has few peers. While he was still in his twenties, his career had been sufficiently varied and spectacular to provide the material for an entire volume of autobiography entitled *Wrong Again, Dan!* The following can only hint at his distinguished range of achievements.

On the way to India in 1944 to join his regiment he lost all his underwear and his only pair of pyjamas while washing them out of the porthole. All the ship's cutlery went the same way when he threw out a basin of dishwater. The troops had to eat with their fingers for the rest of the voyage.

On arrival he was instantly accused of murder. The case foundered only when he pointed at his supposed victim grinning cheerfully in a growing crowd of onlookers.

So enthusiastic was his performance during tests for a commission that after the obstacle course he had to wait for other less interesting candidates to finish so they could come back and rescue him from beneath a railway sleeper.

While in charge of three amphibious weasel tanks, he lost all of them in one week. Two got stuck in a pond and one went through the wall of his own accommodation.

For one so exquisitely disaster prone, a career in explosives was the inevitable course. After an intense period of training he arrived at the South Pacific to blow up some coral reef, never having attempted it before. His finest hour came when he moored his own boat to the very bit of reef that was receiving his closest attention.

'One likes to think there are people who have been worse, but admittedly it does seem unlikely,' says the great man.

The Worst Submarine

The conventional submarine, rising and descending at will, is of only limited interest to our sort of student. It does not compare with the more versatile K-boats which the British developed in 1917.

K-1 sank after colliding with K-4 off the Danish coast. K-2 caught fire on its first test dive. K-3 plunged inexplicably to the seabed with the Prince of Wales on board, eventually resurfacing only to sink after being rammed by K-6. K-4 ran aground; K-5 foundered in the Bay of Biscay.

K-14 sprang a leak before its first trial and during one celebrated manoeuvre in the North Sea it collided with K-22, which used to be K-13, but was renamed after it keeled over at Loch Gare in Scotland while on seaworthiness trials. K-14 sank, while K-22 was damaged beyond repair after getting in the way of HMS *Inflexible*, a cruiser that happened to be passing.

In the same manoeuvre K-17 was struck by HMS *Fearless*, having already been hit by K-7, thereby incapacitating itself. On observing this mayhem, K-4 stopped engines, altered course and was rammed by K-6 which later got stuck on the ocean bed. Better still, K-15 sank in Portsmouth harbour before going anywhere or doing anything.

Ks 18, 19, 20 and 21 were never completed, but their keels were modified for use in the new M range. M-1 was rammed by a merchant vessel while on diving patrol in the Channel and M-2 sank after springing a leak.

The Least Successful Air Attack

To celebrate 'Air Force Week' in 1975, thirty Peruvian fighter planes took part in a demonstration attack on fourteen old fishing boats.

These ramshackle old vessels were sailed out off the coast of Peru and abandoned as targets.

Then the impressive fighter force flew over the craft, high and low, strafing and bombing for the best part of fifteen minutes. To the amazement of the watching crowd, they failed to sink a single boat.

The Worst General

Some men can steal victory from almost certain defeat. Major-General Ambrose Everett Burnside usually progressed in exactly the opposite direction. No advantage, numerical or tactical, was so great that 'Burn', as he was affectionately known, could not throw it away in seconds.

During the American Civil War, Burnside had twelve thousand troops at his disposal. At the Battle of Antietam he overcame this advantage by ordering them to march in single file across an exposed bridge on which enemy guns were trained in large numbers. Only later did he learn that the river was waist deep and could have been forded without danger at any point.

Two years later Burn planned to dynamite a trench along which his men could run in safety into the middle of the enemy camp. As the smoke was clearing his soldiers ran in only to find that they could not climb out again at the other end. The Confederate troops were more than surprised suddenly to find the whole enemy trapped at their feet in a six-foot pit.

On hearing of this manoeuvre President Lincoln said, 'Only Burnside could have managed such a coup, wringing one last spectacular defeat from the jaws of victory.'

The Fastest Defeat in a War

The fastest defeat in any war was in 1896 and entirely thanks to Said Khalid, the pretender Sultan of Zanzibar, and his magnificent forces, which were routed in 36 minutes.

On 27 August the British battle fleet arrived to deliver an ultimatum. The Sultan declined to vacate the palace and so fighting broke out at 9.02 a.m. It reached its peak around 9.15 and was all over by 9.40.

The jewel of the Zanzibar defence force was its only warship, an ageing ocean tramp called the *Glasgow*. This was sunk with only two shells. Furthermore, the Sultan's palace was completely destroyed and the British asked local residents to pay for the ammunition used in wrecking the place.

The Soldiers Who Fought the Second World War Longest

Lieutenant Hiroo Onoda of the Japanese army fought the Second World War until 3 p.m. on 10 March 1974, despite the continued absence of armed opposition in the later years. He used to come out of the jungle on his remote island in the Philippines and fire the odd bullet on behalf of Emperor Hirohito.

In 1945 'come home' letters were dropped from the air, but he ignored them, believing it was just a Yankee trick to make him surrender. After he was found in 1974 it took more than six months to convince him that the war was really over.

But even after this surrender the Second World War still continued on the island of Morotai where Private Teruo Nakamura maintained unbending resistance to the Allied forces. This Indonesian island was finally liberated nine months later in December 1974.

The Country That Fought Two World Wars Simultaneously

When drawing up the Versailles peace treaty at the end of the First World War, the great powers completely forgot about Andorra and failed to include it. Since the regular army of this tiny Pyrenean state comprised only one officer, six privates and four general staff, Andorra was perhaps the country least able to continue the First World War on its own.

It did not possess either artillery or machine-guns, but all soldiers wore on their uniforms buttons that read, 'Touch me if you dare' – the national motto.

Andorra's position worsened in 1939, when it found itself fighting a Second World War as well.

Finally, on 25 September, it signed a private peace treaty with Germany officially concluding the First World War, if not the Second. Its current defence budget is spent entirely on blank ammunition for ceremonial purposes.

The Least Successful Torpedo

In times of war self-sacrifice is a paramount virtue. New heights were achieved in 1941 by HMS *Trinidad* when it fired a torpedo at a passing German destroyer. While sailing in the Arctic, its crew completely overlooked the effect of the icy water on oil in the torpedo's steering mechanism.

The crew watched as it travelled at forty knots towards its target and slowly became aware that the torpedo was starting to follow a curved course. In less than a minute it was pursuing a semi-circular route straight into the *Trinidad*'s path.

Displaying the precision on which naval warfare depends, the torpedo scored a direct hit on the ship's engine room and put HMS *Trinidad* out of action for the rest of the war.

The Least Successful Weapons

The British contribution to this category was the number 74 (ST) hand grenade, known affectionately in the Second World War as the 'sticky bomb'. A special feature was an adhesive coating, which enabled it to stick to the side of an enemy tank. This also enabled it to stick to the thrower, which was generally what happened.

However, the prize for the most useless weapon of all time goes to the Russians, who, rather dourly, invented the dog mine. The plan here was to train dogs to associate food with the underneath of tanks, in the hope that they would run hungrily beneath advancing German Panzer divisions. Bombs were then strapped to their backs.

After a long training process, they associated food solely with Russian tanks and forced an entire Soviet division into retreat. The plan was abandoned on day two of the Russian involvement in the Second World War.

The Least Successful Target Practice

As part of a training exercise off Portsmouth in 1947, the destroyer HMS *Saintes* was required to fire at a target pulled across its bows by the tug *Buccaneer*.

It fired a shell, missed the target and sank the tug.

The Worst Tactician

During the Mexican-American War (1846–1848) General Antonio Lopez De Santa Anna lost every battle he fought, despite having modelled himself closely on Napoleon.

In one inspired 'surprise attack' he dressed all his troops in enemy uniforms. The chaos was indescribable.

During skirmishes with the Texans in the 1830s he was once taken prisoner by them, but in a move of tactical brilliance they released him. On 20 April 1836, showing the calmness of a great commander, he set up camp at the San Jacinto river overlooking a wood where Texans were known to be hiding and ordered his troops to take a siesta.

His entire army was routed in only eighteen minutes while he himself slept.

Although he lacked Napoleon's strategic sense, he did have the same haircut. Otherwise the similarities were few. The Frenchman was short and fat, while Santa Anna was tall, skinny and had only one leg (he had lost the other in 1838 fighting the French and later held a special burial service for it at Santa Paula Cemetery which was attended by a large number wishing to pay their respects).

The Worst Arms Expert

Nazi troops overran the armoury at Brest in 1940 and captured a new French secret weapon, the 15-inch 'Richelieu' gun. The delighted German high command immediately put an arms expert to work investigating this new weapon, which, they believed, could swing the war their way if put to use quickly.

However, our expert was not to be rushed. Nothing if not thorough, he finally handed over a thick dossier, detailing every aspect of the gun's usage and capabilities in April 1944. The report also announced that it would be impossible to use the gun in the remaining months of the war because he had used up all the available ammunition in conducting his tests.

The Most Unsuccessful Nine-Gun Salute

In 1974 the Royal Navy entered the yacht *Adventure* for the Round-the-World Yacht Race. The 55-foot boat had just won the previous leg of the race and when it rounded Cape Horn it was decided that HMS *Endurance* would welcome it with a nine-gun salute.

The sixth shot hit the yacht and wrecked its headsails. The ten-man crew had to spend the rest of the day sewing them up.

The Worst Ever Duel

For many years the duel fought between Sir Hierome Sankey and Sir William Petty in 1645 was without equal. The dispute arose in London over a matter of honour now lost in the mists of time.

Sir Hierome was a tough character and Sir William, being of a nervous disposition, was reluctant to fight him.

Since Sir Hierome had initiated the duel, Sir William had the choice of venue and weapons. Brilliantly, he chose a pitch-dark cellar and two carpenters' axes, which neither of them could lift.

This stood as the worst until December 1971, when the duel between a Uruguayan field marshal and a fellow general quite surpassed it. This occurred when the field marshal called his colleague a 'socialist'. They decided to settle the matter honourably.

Meeting at dawn in one of Montevideo's public parks, the two soldiers fired 37 rounds at each other from a distance of 25 paces. Neither man was hurt.

The field marshal's second said they had failed to put on their glasses before commencing their back-to-back walk.

The Least Bellicose War

Outraged by the news that King Alphonso XII had been insulted during his state visit to Paris, the Mayor of Lijar, a small town in southern Spain, declared war on France.

While the three hundred citizens backed his passionate call to arms, nobody was entirely certain what to do next. Not a single shot was fired, although the Mayor, Don Miguel Garcia Saez, nonetheless became known as 'the terror of the Sierras' for this exploit.

Ninety-three years later King Juan Carlos, Alphonso's grandson, made a visit to France that went off without a hitch. In 1981 the town council of Lijar decided that 'in view of the excellent attitude of the French', it would be safe to suspend hostilities.

The Least Successful Undercover Operation

Two undercover agents from the Spanish Civil Guard spent an evening in 1975 trailing three extremely suspicious-looking characters around Vittoria. At midnight they followed them into a Basque nightclub.

They crossed the dance floor and were just going to pounce when the dubious trio sprang up, put them into half nelsons and frogmarched them out of the building.

The three were undercover agents from the Spanish Civil Guard who had been following the other two all night on the grounds that they looked extremely suspicious.

The Least Successful Manoeuvre

New standards for reversing into a jetty were set on 17 May 1966 by the Royal Navy frigate HMS *Ulster*. During training exercises in the Tamar estuary at Plymouth its starboard engine control became stuck in the 'half-astern' position. Attempts to free it only jammed the handle on 'full astern'. The engine room obeyed the order and soon the ship was gathering speed and sailing backwards straight for a stone jetty.

The captain telephoned the engine room, but there was no reply. He then ordered both the anchors to be dropped in an attempt to slow the ship down and sent his officer of the watch down to the engine room to tell them what was happening. On the way there he met the entire ship's company going in the opposite direction to emergency stations. He was unable to make any headway.

The frigate eventually hit the jetty travelling at 8 knots. The impact shortened the ship by seven feet and compressed the air inside it. This caused the only casualty. A sailor who was halfway through a hatch at the moment of impact was shot fifteen feet into the air and landed safely on the jetty.

The Least Successful Attempt to Opt Out

Fearing another world war, a Canadian pacifist decided to sell his home and move to a quiet part of the planet

where peace was guaranteed. After months of delibera-
tion he chose the remotest and safest spot in the atlas.

In March 1982 he moved to the Falkland Islands, just
five days before the Argentinians invaded this island,
marking the start of the Falklands War.

7

PLAYING THE GAME

The Highest Score for One Golf Hole
The Worst Matador
The Least Successful Jockey
The Most Knocked-out Boxer
The Worst Goalkeeper
The Fastest Own Goal
The Worst Batsman
The Heaviest Ever Cricket Defeat
The Worst Football Team
The Least Enthusiastic Football Team
The Heaviest Football Defeat
The Worst Basketball Team
The Worst Behaved Rugby Match
The Least Disciplined Football Teams
The Least Successful Attempt at Crowd Control
The Least Successful Cricket Match
The Lowest Score in a Test Match
The Worst Save

'Nice guys come last.'
AMOS ALONZO STAGG

The Highest Score for One Golf Hole

In 1912 an American enthusiast made golfing history when she took 166 strokes over a 130-yard hole.

During the qualifying round of the Shawnee Invitational for Ladies at Shawnee-on-Delaware, Pennsylvania, she confidently approached the sixteenth hole, for which four strokes were normally adequate. Her first shot, however, sent the ball into the Binnickill river, an obstacle many would regard as final.

When she saw that it floated, she boarded a rowing boat, with her husband at the oars and herself at the prow, wielding a golf club. For one and a half miles her husband rowed and kept count of the occasions on which his wife had cause to swipe at it.

Eventually, she beached the thing and made her way back through a forest. Fellow competitors had given up hope of ever seeing her again, when they heard the cry of 'fore' and saw the ball fly onto the green from a totally unexpected direction. She completed the hole in just under two hours.

The Worst Matador

Rafael Gomez was one of those rare matadors in whose company a bull was often safer than in the hands of a vet. Once, when asked what he did to train, he replied, 'Smoke Havana cigars.' In 1911 he astonished spectators at the Seville bullring when he fought a bull while sitting on a chair.

Known as 'El Gallo', he would stride into the ring manfully, throw a flower at a local beauty and then dedicate the bull to her in a long and florid speech. 'To thee alone I dedicate the life of this bull,' he would say before turning round to strike a fine pose and await the opposition. As soon as the bull snorted into sight, El Gallo would regularly drop his cape, sprint across the ring and dive headlong over the barrier in a move known technically as an *espantada*. 'All of us artists have bad days,' the unique matador used to say.

He was sometimes panic stricken simply because of the way the bull looked at him. Ernest Hemingway said that for a bull to kill El Gallo would be 'in bad taste'.

He was brought out of retirement seven times by popular demand. In his last fight, on 10 October 1918, El Gallo dedicated the bull to no fewer than three dignitaries in his longest ever speech and, after all this, he refused to kill it because it had winked at him. Eventually his brother had to kill it to save the family honour.

The Least Successful Jockey

Few jockeys have been more regularly parted from their horse than the Duke of Albuquerque.

In 1963 he made racing history when bookies offered

odds of 66–1 against his finishing the Grand National on horseback. Dividing his time equally between the saddle and the stretcher, this Spanish aristocrat entered the National seven times with consistently impressive results.

Generally, he would start with the others, gallop briefly and then wake up in the intensive care unit of the Royal Liverpool Infirmary. It was the fences that caused the trouble.

In 1952 the Duke fell at the sixth fence and almost broke his neck. In 1963 it was the fourth. In 1965 his horse collapsed and in 1973 his stirrup broke. He clung on bravely for eight fences before being sent into inevitable orbit.

In 1974 he fell off during training and staff at the casualty unit were surprised to see him wheeled in before the race had even begun. Undeterred, this fine man rode in the National with a broken collarbone and a leg in plaster.

'I sat like sack of potatoes,' he said, explaining his technique, 'and gave horse no help.' This may explain how this eminent equestrian came to complete the course for the only time in his splendid career.

The Most Knocked-out Boxer

The boxing ring contains no greater star than Bruce 'The Mouse' Strauss, who has been knocked out more times than anybody else. In his career he hit the canvas on thirty-one occasions at twenty-nine locales. 'A couple

of places like me so much they asked me back for more,'
says Strauss, whom grateful boxers have queued up to
fight.

The most frequently defeated pugilist in the world,
he explains that he is 'not competitive' and 'never got
an emotional charge when the referee raised my hand
as winner'. As *Boxing News* said, this fine man 'knows the
agony of victory and the thrill of defeat'.

According to his sparring partner, Richie Segedin,
Mouse sometimes goes too far. 'Mouse always goes too
far actually. I've seen him drink a beer that a fan offered
him – during the fight. And he tries to chat up round-
card girls while they walk around the ring.' Once, when
knocked out, he feigned extensive injury so that he could
stay in hospital for two months and court a nurse who
later became Mrs Mouse.

In 1986 Strauss says he rang the Associated Press
Agency to announce his retirement, but they had 'absolutely no interest'.

Part of Strauss's record-breaking achievement is due
to the fact that he fought an astronomical number of
professional bouts, two of them on the same night, and
many under an assumed name or cunningly disguised
with dyed hair or a false moustache.

The Worst Goalkeeper

In these days of defensive play it is the general cry that
not enough goals are scored. No one has done more to

change this situation than Chris Smith, the outstanding goalkeeper of Worthing Boys' Club in 1983.

In only eighteen matches this entertaining player let through 647 goals, an average of 35.9 per game. There were, of course, some days when he did much better than this (he once let in nearer fifty, five of them in seven minutes). 'I don't always see the ball,' he said. 'It goes through my legs.'

Alarmingly, he was sent on a special training course, but his natural gifts could not be tampered with.

If there had been a net on the goalposts and he had not been forced to walk miles picking the ball up each time there is no telling what this fine boy might have achieved.

The Fastest Own Goal

In an electrifying start to their match on 3 January 1977, Torquay United set an example that no other league side has equalled. Cambridge United kicked off and Ian Seddon struck a high ball down the length of the pitch, whereupon the brilliant Torquay centre half, Pat Kruse, leaped above his own defence with lightning reactions. He headed the ball into his own net after only six seconds, scoring the fastest own goal in the history of league football.

A lesser team would have settled for that, but Torquay were on top form. In the forty-ninth minute they increased Cambridge's lead when their full back, Phil

Sandercock, powered a spectacular header past his own goalkeeper, Tony Lee, who had been untroubled by Cambridge attacks.

In the second half Torquay slumped and drew level.

The Worst Batsman

Although Patrick Moore, the astronomer, has had some success as a bowler, thanks to his 'medium-paced leg-breaks with a long, leaping, kangaroo-type action', we are prepared to overlook this in view of his immense contribution to the art of batting.

In a playing career which extends over half a century with the Lord's Taverners and his village team in Sussex, he has achieved a superb batting average of 0.8 runs an innings and has broken into double figures only once since 1949.

In his best season (1948) he scored only one run and that was from a dropped catch. That year he shattered the existing record for the most consecutive ducks (a measly eight) when he powered to a magnificent eighteen on the trot.

There are two possible explanations for his prowess. Mr Moore himself puts it down to having only two strokes, 'a cow shot to leg' and 'a desperate forward swat', which he uses in strict rotation. Furthermore, he does not wear spectacles when batting. 'Someone said it wouldn't make any difference if I wore binoculars.'

The Heaviest Ever Cricket Defeat

The most important team in the history of first-class cricket is the Dera Ismail Khan XI of Pakistan. Between 2 and 4 December 1964 they played an Ayub Trophy fixture at Lahore against a run-crazed Railways XI who batted until lunchtime on the third day. It was one dreary, predictable six after another for hours on end until they were all out for 851.

Out came Dera Ismail Khan in fine fettle. In no time the game was alive with thrills and excitement. Their first innings was a model of economy (they were all out for 32) and in the second innings they were all out for an even more thrilling 27 to achieve the heaviest defeat in the history of the game.

The Worst Football Team

Thanks to the tremendous enthusiasm of boys, this is one of our most hotly contested categories. In 1972 the Norwich Nomads seemed to have it sewn up after a splendid season during which they lost all twenty of their games in the Norwich Boys League, scoring 11 goals and letting in 431 (an average of 21.55 goals conceded per game).

Their mantle was taken over in the 1983 season by the all-conquering Worthing Boys' Club under-twelve team, which also lost all their games in the season but scored only 6 goals for with an impressive 647 against (an average of 35.9 goals let in per game: see *The Worst Goalkeeper* above). Widely hailed as the worst team in the country, they were given the annual Worthing award by the mayor for generating national interest in the town. Five years later, they had still not won a game.

The Least Enthusiastic Football Team

Blackburn Rovers showed definitive sporting reluctance in their game against Burnley in 1891. In almost perfect conditions (it had been snowing steadily for three hours before kick-off and few fans bothered to turn up) Blackburn let in goals every quarter of an hour and were 3–0 down at half-time.

When the interval went on an unusually long time, it became clear that Blackburn Rovers did not want to come out at all. Eventually, their team straggled onto the pitch, but the crowd could not help noticing that there were only seven of them.

Ten minutes later, Lofthouse of Blackburn had smacked the face of the Burnley captain, who retaliated with a punch. Both players were sent off. Feeling that this was an extremely good idea, the entire Blackburn team decided to follow them, with the exception of the goalkeeper, a Mr Arthur, who remained at his post.

The referee, Mr Clegg, waited a few moments in the hope that Blackburn Rovers might reappear. When they failed to do so, the game restarted with the entire Burnley team bearing down upon Mr Arthur. Nichols scored for Burnley, but the goalkeeper successfully claimed it was offside and the referee abandoned the match.

The Blackburn captain later explained that this was not a protest against Lofthouse being sent off. They simply wanted to join him and were quite happy for Burnley to have the two points.

The Heaviest Football Defeat

The public flock to football matches in the hope of seeing goals scored. Thanks to Bon Accord Football Club, Scottish fans saw the greatest match ever played in the British Isles.

This entertaining side from Aberdeen let in thirty-six spectacular goals during a cup tie against Arbroath on 19 September 1885. It was the largest number ever conceded in the professional game.

The Bon Accord defence played throughout with a wonderfully open style that thrilled the happy crowd. A mere ten goals down at the interval, they wasted much time keeping the ball in midfield. But in the second half they got into their stride and dominated the play with their unselfish passing of the ball. Soon they had let in fifteen goals.

After sixty minutes a Bon Accord player came close to marring the whole game with their only shot at goal. Fortunately, it was intercepted by Collie of Arbroath.

The whistle went shortly after the thirty-sixth goal and Bon Accord trooped off to become the talking point of all Scotland. In an admiring report the local paper said they 'never seemed dismayed by the turn of events'. And rightly so. As the editorial went on to observe, 'It was the most amusing game ever seen in Arbroath.'

The Worst Basketball Team

Friendsville Academy Foxes notched up 128 consecutive defeats between 1967 and 1973, a record unequalled in the history of basketball. Their coach says he used to give them pep talks until he 'discovered it was making them nervous'.

In 1970 Phil Patterson was named as Foxville's outstanding player. When Douglas S. Looney from the *National Observer* pointed out that Mr Patterson had not scored a single point, the coach replied, 'You don't think scoring is everything, do you?'

In his report Mr Looney gives the following verbatim account of their conversation:

Looney: Is there anything this team does well?

Coach: Not really.

Looney: Are you making any progress?

Coach: I couldn't truthfully say that we are.

Looney: Do you like coaching?

Coach: I don't care that much for basketball.

Their greatest feat was 71–0 and their closest was 2–0, a scoreline ensured by a Friendsville player putting the ball in his own basket.

In no time they were, of course, nationally famous.

('There hasn't been so much excitement since the Baptist Church burned down.') So celebrated did they become that their mascot's fox suit was stolen by souvenir hunters.

Prominent in their gym were signs saying, 'Character not victory is the important thing' and 'Humble in victory, praiseworthy in defeat.' The scene of unrelieved praiseworthiness at Foxville was disturbed only by their sole remaining cheerleader, Miss Patti Walsh, who kept bouncing up and down, shouting unhelpful slogans concerning the onward march to victory.

The Worst Behaved Rugby Match

The game between Abingdon and Didcot on 5 January 1983 went straight into the record books when the referee, Police Sergeant Peter Richmond, sent both teams off with five minutes left to play.

He blew his whistle, pointed to the dressing room, walked off muttering 'I've had enough of this', got into his car and drove away to write a blistering report for the Oxfordshire Rugby Union. It was the first time in the game's history that 100 per cent marching orders had been issued.

According to the players, there had been 'a bit of a scuffle'.

The Least Disciplined Football Teams

Competition here is intense. On 2 February 1975 the entire Glencraig United football team and their two substitutes were all booked before they had even left the dressing room. The referee, a Mr Tarbet of Bearsden, took exception to the chants that greeted his arrival.

In November 1969 all twenty-two players, including one who went to hospital, were booked in the match between Tongham Youth and Hawley, which one of the players later described as 'a good hard game'. Rising to his task, the referee, John McAdam, then booked a linesman for dissent. 'At one stage in the match he threw the flag on the floor and after that never seemed to have the same interest in the game.'

Some claim that this was the wildest game ever played, but such people were not present on 25 February 1951 when the Lily Mills FC met the Ukrainian Sports Club, Rochdale, in the first round of the local charity cup. The referee not only ordered both teams off, but also cautioned the crowd who had joined in the melee.

The Least Successful Attempt at Crowd Control

The powerful effects of tear gas were fully displayed in October 1987 during an African league soccer match between Gor Mahia and AFC Leopard. Trouble broke out when a Gor Mahia official went on to the pitch and refused to leave it, despite complaints from the opposition that he was using witchcraft to influence the game.

In the confusion that followed, twenty-two players, eight members of the training staff and a large section of the crowd joined in a fist-swinging free-for-all on the pitch. Taking firm action, the police raced on with tear gas, but were themselves overwhelmed and had to be carried off by the team, having made no arrests. Witchcraft prevailed and Gor Mahia won 1–0.

The Least Successful Cricket Match

At the start of the twentieth century grown men were put to shame by two schoolboy teams in Cambridge. The match brought together King's College Choir School and Trophy Boys XI.

Trophy Boys won the toss, batted first and were out for nought. Then King's went in and Trophy's first delivery was a no ball.

This gave the King's Choir School a score of one and victory in the only known cricket match with no runs whatsoever.

The Lowest Score in a Test Match

New Zealand achieved this unique honour in March 1955 when they scored a spectacular 26 against England at Auckland.

It is worth listing the scores of the eleven great bats-
men who shared the glory.

J. G. Leggatt	1
M. B. Poore	0
B. Sutcliffe	11
J. R. Reid	1
G. O. Rathbone	7
S. N. McGregor	1
H. B. Cave	5
A. R. MacGibbon	0
I. A. Colquhoun	0
A. M. Moir (not out)	0
J. A. Hayes	0
Extras	0
Total	26

The Worst Save

This honour falls to Isadore Irandir of the Brazilian
team Rio Preto, who let in a goal after three seconds.

From the kick-off in the soccer match between Cor-
inthians and Rio Preto at Bahia Stadium, the ball was
passed to Roberto Rivelino, who scored instantly with a
left-foot drive from the halfway line. The ball went past
the ear of Senhor Irandir while he was on his knees finishing pre-match prayers in the goalmouth.

8

THE CULTURAL EXPLOSION

The Worst Singer
The Worst Ever Novelist
The Worst Poet
The Least Successful Songwriter
The Worst Long-Playing Record
The Worst Films
The Worst Poet Laureate
The Dud Book Fair
The Least Satisfactory Performance of
The Sound of Music
The Least Successful Feminist Book
The Worst Poem Ever Written
The Worst Music Critic
The Critic Who Reviewed the Wrong Show

'And now, kind friends, what I have
wrote, I hope you will pass o'er.
And not criticise as some have done
Hitherto herebefore.'

JULIA MOORE

The Worst Singer

The glory of the human voice has never had fuller expression than in the career of Florence Foster Jenkins.

La Jenkins was not apologetically low key in her badness. She was defiantly and gloriously dreadful. No one, before or since, has succeeded in liberating themselves quite so completely from the shackles of musical notation. Opera was her medium and she squawked heroically through the best-known arias with a refreshing abandon.

From her birth in Pennsylvania in 1864 to her debut forty years later, it is fair to say that neither her parents nor her husband gave the slightest encouragement to her musical ambitions.

Then papa left her his fortune and, with this newfound wealth and freedom, she launched her assault on the musical world.

Her flair for the dress design fully equalled her singing gift and, in any concert, thrilled audiences were treated to a minimum of three costume changes. One minute she would appear sporting an immense pair of wings to render 'Ave Maria'. The next she would emerge in the garb of a señorita, with a rose between her teeth and a basket full of flowers, to unload her Spanish showstopper, 'Cavelitos'.

In this song she would punctuate each verse by hurling rosebuds into the audience. Once she hurled the basket as well.

The audience could always tell when she was going to grant an encore. She would dispatch her overworked accompanist Cosmé McMoon out into the auditorium to collect up the flowers so that she might repeat her triumph.

On 26 October 1944 she hired and filled to capacity the Carnegie Hall in New York for her farewell appearance. She started disappointingly with three correct notes, but her admirers need not have feared. Before long she abandoned pitch, stave and key and was as out of tune as it is possible to be without coming back in tune again.

The Worst Ever Novelist

In the 1940s ardent admirers claimed that Mrs Amanda McKittrick Ros was the worst novelist in English or any other language. Nothing has happened since to alter this happy state of affairs. Born in 1861, Amanda Malvina Fitzalan Anna Margaret McLelland McKittrick Ros was also the manager of the local lime kiln.

Blessed with the gift of alluring alliteration, this Belfast housewife wrote four novels: *Delina Delaney*, *Irene Iddesleigh*, *Donald Dudley* and *Helen Huddleson* (in which Lord Raspberry pays unwanted attentions to a country girl). On a typical day characters such as Rodney Rupert, Oscar Otwell and Marjorie Mason feel able to say, 'Leave me now deceptive demon of deluded mockery. Lurk no more around the vale of vanity, like a vindictive viper.'

Her style was full of such burning intensity that mere sense was rarely allowed to interfere with it. Her characters never sit in a room, they are 'sharing its midst'; nothing is ever white – female hands, passing clouds and certain tablecloths are always 'snowy', and troublesome women are 'most retorting'. Trousers, meanwhile, are 'the southern necessity'. She is also extremely fond of the word 'mushroom', which appears more often than is strictly required.

With the constraints of grammar she would have no truck. The following is a typical example:

> Her uncle replied 'Ah dear Helen, I feel heartsick of
> this frivolous frittery fraternity of fragiles flitting round
> and about Earth's huge plane wearing their morning
> livery of religion as a cloak of design tainted with the
> milk of mockery,' wiping his moistened brow with a
> crimson handkerchief, while Helen acquiesced, Henry
> Jnr remaining silent.

She was a stout woman given to black hairnets, who had the words 'at home always to the honourable' printed on her calling cards. Rightly convinced of her own genius, she condemned all critics of her work as donkeyosities, egotistical earthworms, hog-washing hooligans, critic cads, random hacks of illiteration, talent wipers of the wormy order, the gas-bag section, poking hounds, poisonous apes, maggoty numbskulls, evil-minded snapshots of spleen and, worst of all, the mushroom class of idiotics.

Although her novels were unforgivably out of print soon after publication, she said, 'I feel I am a great favourite as a writer. I will be talked about at the end of a thousand years. I afford pleasure and give satisfaction to the million and one who continually thirst for aught from my pen. I also know I write different from any known writer organiser of prose.' She also wrote poetry (see *The Worst Poet*).

The Worst Poet

Having exhausted the possibilities of the novel, Amanda McKittrick Ros turned her talents to the poetic field. She produced two volumes, entitled *Poems of Puncture* and *Fumes of Formation*.

The remarkable thing about her poetry was its range. She could write religious verse, as in her 'Ode to Easter': 'Dear Lord, the day of eggs is here.'

And in 'The Engineer Divine' she discusses the possibility of an electrified railway to heaven:

> The current of faith from the battery of prayer
> Can act on the magnet of love.
> With movements produced by a Motor Divine
> Which matchless perfection displays,
> The engine of Truth as it runs up the line
> The Train of Salvation conveys.

As a war poet, she had similar conviction:

> We know you'll do your duty and come to a little harm
> And if you meet the Kaiser, cut off his other arm.

Her descriptive verse was also able to capture the spirit of a place, as in her reflective lines on Poets' Corner at Westminster Abbey:

> Holy Moses! Take a look!
> Flesh decayed in every nook
> Some rare bits of brain lie here,
> Mortal loads of beef and beer.

When in more savage mood, she launched vitriolic attacks on lawyers. She wrote an entire poem, for example, denouncing Mickey 'Monkeyface' McBlear, a local solicitor who had the audacity to represent her opponents in a lawsuit.

Above all, Mrs Ros was a moralist. In her poem 'I Love to See a Lady Nice and Natural at Any Price' she inveighs against the modern woman who behaves like a man:

> and smoke and spit, no matter where,
> and very often curse and swear,
> I lose my temper o'er these arts
> That stamp such women – Dirty Clarts.

The Least Successful Songwriter

For twenty years Mr Geoffrey O'Neill has been writing what he calls 'good catchy tunes that people remember and whistle'. In this time he has composed 501 songs and three musicals. Not one of them has been recorded, published or performed by professionals.

Mr O'Neill, who comes from Great Dunmow in Essex, files all his songs away in case there should be a sudden demand for them. He cheerfully reports that song number 102 is called 'Try, Try Again', while number 332 is entitled 'People Think I'm Stupid'. An oil firm employee, he gives public lectures on how unsuccessful his songs are.

The Worst Long-Playing Record

One of the most popular LPs of 1978 was *The World's Worst Record Show*, which brought together thirty of the worst pop songs ever recorded.

Three of the tracks were by Jess Conrad. One of them, 'Cherry Pie', is concerned with likening his loved one to a fruit-filled pastry. Another asks 'Why Am I Living?' to an insistent backing of 'Wo dah dah yip yip'.

In the barely comprehensible 'Transfusion', Nervous Norvus records his continuing debt to blood donors in the light of his predilection for speeding.

The most reassuringly pointless song is Steve Bent's 'I'm Going to Spain'. Accompanied by maracas, he gives musical justification for his holiday plans revolving around the fact that 'cousin Norman had a real fine time last year'.

The worst is the contribution by the Legendary Stardust Cowboy who yells, screams, bawls, howls, bays, whoops, yelps, shouts and wails without one word ever being comprehensible, until drowned out by demonic drum and trumpet solos that defy description, all under the name of 'Paralysed'.

Naturally, the LP was a great hit and sold 25,000 copies a week in the London area alone.

The Worst Films

In the history of the cinema the World's Worst Film Festival in 1980 proved a high spot. The programme for this treasure house of special celluloid moments got off to a cracking start with *Tiny Town*, the world's first all-midget Western. It consisted mainly of cowboys walking under saloon doors, chasing each other round bar-room table legs and riding into the sunset on what were obviously Shetland ponies.

Applause broke out in the chase sequence when the three-foot-nine hero 'Rocky' Curtis pursued a three-foot-eight villain, Little Billy. He galloped out of town on a black horse, and was next seen scooting along on a white one, only to arrive at his ranch reunited with the black one.

For six days the festival maintained this high standard and special acclaim went to *The Attack of the Killer Tomatoes*, a four-hour epic in which a consignment of giant tomatoes goes berserk and terrorises San Diego. In one of the best scenes a housewife is threatened by a bloodthirsty seedless oozing out of her in-sink garbage-grinding unit.

The eventual winner was *They Saved Hitler's Brain*, in which the Führer's grey cells wreak post-bunker havoc on a scale that would have surprised even Adolf.

The Worst Poet Laureate

At the end of the nineteenth century Joseph Gwyer set himself up as the unofficial poet laureate of Britain. Why, he reasoned, should the Queen have only one of these when he himself had ample free time from his work as a potato salesman in Penge to perform such literary services?

For this task he had three main qualifications. First, he had no access to state occasions of any kind. Second, it goes without saying that he was unblighted at birth by literary gifts. And, third, he had a rigorous poetic honesty so that if things were too hard for him to describe, he would quite simply say so.

At one procession featuring the Prince of Wales he wrote:

> At evening too the dazzled light
> Illumed [*sic*] the darkness of the night
> I can't paint it for reasons best,
> Twas grand, though I in crowd was pressed

For twenty years he bombarded members of the royal family with his accounts of their doings, which elicited curt and frosty letters of acknowledgement from their private secretaries.

Undeterred by this coolness, Gwyer produced in 1875 a volume of his work, entitled *Poems (Commended by Royalty)*, in which he included all of these frosty letters by way of recommendation. On the title page he further announced that he could also send, on a sale-or-return basis, sacks of potatoes and, indeed, gilt-framed photographs of himself and his carthorse.

This book includes his timeless lines upon the funeral of Dr Livingstone, which he did not actually attend:

> Heap on more grass was his request
> As hapless now he laid to rest.

It also contains an 'Ode on the Visit of the Shah of Persia', which is largely devoted to his teetotal enthusiasm:

> Intoxicating drafts he never does drink
> If this we copied should we not be better, think?

When reviewing his collected works, the *New York Tribune* said that young people wavering between Mr Gwyer's poetry and his potatoes should unhesitatingly choose the latter.

The Dud Book Fair

A record number of visitors poured into the 1982 York Book Fair, probably because its central feature was the first 'Dud Books of All Times' exhibition. Never before had such a powerful collection of completely unsaleable volumes been gathered together under one roof.

The imposing entrance to the Assembly Rooms was specially decked out for the occasion with vivid wallpaper, fairy lights and a Day-Glo pink signboard.

The most popular book on show was *The List of Stop Cocks in the Liver Building, Liverpool, 1912*. This was closely followed by a signed copy of *The Philosophy of Elbert Hubbard*.

Even before the exhibition opened, one natural-history expert snapped up copies of both *The Common Teasel As a Carnivorous Plant* and *Ostrich Egg-Shell Cups of Mesopotamia in Ancient and Modern Times*.

The early history of sanitation was fully represented by such work as *The Law Relating to Sewers and Drains 1904*, while the travel section included *Uganda for a Holiday* by Sir Frederick Treves and *The Little I Saw of Cuba* by Burr McIntosh.

In the biography and memoir department *The Mother of Goethe* made a happy companion to *I Was Hitler's Aunt*. *Heroes and Heroines of Libya* was a huge hit, as was *Jokes Cracked by Lord Aberdeen* in a tartan cover. The only disappointment was that the promised copy of *The Romance of Leprosy* by E. Mackerchar did not materialise.

The Least Satisfactory Performance of *The Sound of Music*

Only the South Koreans have really got to grips with *The Sound of Music*, the well-known film in which Julie Andrews and a selection of carbolically scrubbed infants burst into song up Alps, inside monasteries, on assorted staircases and in a wide range of wholly surprising locations.

Finding the film a shade over long, the Koreans wisely decided to cut out all the songs. Shown with no music whatsoever, yet still called *The Sound of Music,* the film proved extremely popular and played to full houses all over South-East Asia.

The Least Successful Feminist Book

Virago Books launched in 1987 a new series of feminist books for teenagers. In the first batch was *Down the Road, Worlds Away* by Ranila Khan, whom the publishers described as 'an unknown Islamic author'. It was a sensitive collection of short stories showing the problems that Asian girls face growing up in an oppressive, male-dominated society.

The book was withdrawn soon after publication when Virago discovered that it was, in fact, written by an unknown Anglican vicar called the Reverend Toby Forward, who afterwards explained that he 'did it because people often don't take Anglican vicars all that seriously'.

The Worst Poem Ever Written

Although this is a highly subjective matter, there is a strong case for arguing that Mr Theophile Marzial's poem, 'A Tragedy', written in 1837, has never been surpassed.

The Pre-Raphaelite poet had honey-blond hair and caused a stir by saying in a loud voice, 'Am I not the darling of the British Museum Reading Room?', while seated in that very establishment. He once recited this poem in his deep baritone voice at a soirée organised by Dante Gabriel Rossetti, the poet and painter. In the thoughtful silence that followed, Rossetti said it was 'written on a plan absolutely inadmissible'.

The opening stanza establishes the elegiac mood of the poem:

> Death!
> Plop.
> The barges down in the river flop.
> Flop, plop.

After a page or so in this exciting vein Marzials really gets going:

> To the oozy waters that lounge and flop
> On the black scrag-piles, where the loosed cords plop,
> As the raw wind whines in the thin tree-top
> Plop, plop.

Before long he is in top gear:

> At the water that oozes up, plop and plop,
> On the barges that flop
> And dizzy me dead
> I might reel and drop
> Plop
> Dead.

With a tactful reticence that is rare nowadays he does not tell us exactly what his problem is until two-thirds of the way through this lengthy poem. Eventually, it transpires that somebody has gone off with somebody else's fiancée (whose is not clear). However, the fact is recorded in a rising tide of emotion that takes us to the poem's unforgettable conclusion:

> And my head is as empty as air –
>> I can do,
>> I can dare
>> (Plop, plop
>> The barges flop
>> Drip, drop.)
>> I can dare! I can dare!
> And let myself all run away with my head
> And stop.
>> Drop.
>> Dead.
>> Plop, flop.
>>> Plop

Many have puzzled away at the exact meaning of the lines:

> And let myself all run away with my head
> And stop.

But scholars of all nations agree it was a masterpiece.

The Worst Music Critic

Any critic can fail to spot a genius, but only James William Davison had the daunting consistency to miss every single one for an entire century. The great man was editor of *Musical World* magazine (1843–80) in London and his every pronouncement has now been proved wrong by posterity.

In his stimulating career he dismissed Tchaikovsky's *Romeo and Juliet* as 'rubbishy'; said that Verdi's *Rigoletto* would 'flicker and flare for a night or two and then be forgotten', and argued that 'Wagner cannot write music.' He slated *Tannhäuser* as 'commonplace, lumbering and awkward', *The Flying Dutchman* as 'hideous' and *Lohengrin* as 'an incoherent mass of rubbish'. He felt that Liszt was 'talentless funghi', Berlioz was 'more a vulgar lunatic than a healthy musician', and Schumann's entire output was so devoid of melody or form that it 'can hardly be called music at all'.

Schubert got a complete pasting, being 'overrated and literally beneath criticism'. The great critic also felt that Chopin was 'knotty, crude and ill-digested'. His entire works present 'a motley surface of ranting hyperbole and excruciating cacophony' full of clumsy harmonies, sickly melodies and an utter ignorance of design that 'wholly forbid the possibility of Chopin being a skilled or even moderately proficient artist'.

In the whole nineteenth-century scene Davison could detect only one cast-iron genius who would become a household name: Mr Sterndale Bennett. When others scoffed that this choice, the unshakeable critic said, 'Let posterity award to each his real deserts.'

The Critic Who Reviewed the Wrong Show

How necessary is it for a critic to see the production that he is reviewing? Opinions differ on this but Heuwell

Tircuit of the *San Francisco Chronicle* has done much to
further the view that such details only clutter the mind.

In August 1987 this great critic wrote a devastating
attack on the San Francisco Ballet's performance of the
pas de deux from Bizet's opera *La Jolie Fille de Perth*.

In a stimulating tirade, headed 'San Francisco Ballet
Misses a Step', Tircuit hit top gear. 'Either the San Francisco Ballet is being overworked or under-rehearsed,' he
roared. For a start, he was not impressed by the dancers who 'looked a tad dumpy'. He found that David
McNaughton was 'not up to his best'. And, as for Lud-
mila Lopukhova, 'her potato-drenched Russian training
seemed less heavy than in the past. But she, when added
to Tomasson's dank choreography, didn't quite come
through.'

Perhaps this was because the performance was cancelled that night and replaced by *Ballet for Five Male Dancers* in which Miss Lophukova naturally did not appear.

In his report Mr Tircuit estimated that there were ten
thousand people in the audience at the open-air theatre.
His newspaper later estimated that he had not been one
of them. Defending his imaginative review, he said that
he attended the performance, but felt so ill that he was
unaware of what he was watching.

☛ 9 ☚

THE GLORY OF THE STAGE

The Worst Ever Actor
The Least Successful Productions
The Most Lines Forgotten by One Actor
The Worst Ever Variety Act
The Unluckiest Stage Show
The Worst West End Play
The Least Informative Book
The Worst Playwright
The Most Embarrassed Author
The Shortest West End Run

'The best in this kind are but shadows
And the worst are no worse.'
WILLIAM SHAKESPEARE,
A Midsummer Night's Dream, V:1

The Worst Ever Actor

The worst actor ever to appear on a stage anywhere was Robert 'Romeo' Coates (1772–1842). Hardly ever did a production in which he figured end without riot.

His total incapacity to play any part whatsoever, combined with his insistence on wearing diamonds from head to foot, regardless of role, and his tendency to 'improve' on Shakespeare as he went along, made him immensely popular with astonished audiences up and down Britain.

His specialisation was death scenes, which he used to preface by spreading a white silk handkerchief on the stage. These scenes were so protracted and so deliriously received that he frequently did encores, dying again.

Born in the West Indies, the son of a wealthy American sugar planter, he dabbled there in amateur dramatics.

When he inherited the estate at thirty-five, Romeo Coates felt that he needed a larger platform and that he owed it to England to perform there. His belief in his own theatrical genius was unshakeable. Criticism he put down to envy.

He arrived in Bath in 1807 in a diamond-encrusted carriage, shaped like a seashell and emblazoned with a gilt cockerel bearing his appropriate family motto: 'While

I live, I'll crow.' His habit of declaiming 'improved' passages of Shakespeare ('I fancy that is rather better') over breakfast at his inn soon brought him to the attention of the manager of the Theatre Royal.

While Coates awaited his British debut with pleasure, word got around as to the likely standard of his performance and all the tickets sold rapidly.

On that blustery November night he appeared in his greatest role – Romeo – a part that he was later forced to abandon because no actress would agree to play Juliet opposite him.

It started quietly enough but when he entered the audience gave way to ecstatic cheers (which he stopped to acknowledge). Visually, Coates was always surprising and, on this occasion, he chose to dress his Romeo in a spangled sky-blue coat, bright crimson pantaloons and a white hat, excessively trimmed with feathers. Over all this was spattered a multitude of diamonds and the total effect ran quite counter to Shakespeare's description of the character as a 'quiet, virtuous and well-governed youth'.

The play continued in a hail of orange peel and whenever the audience crowed 'cock-a-doodle-do' at Coates, he would break off, regardless of Juliet on the balcony, and crow back at them.

At one point the audience joined in a delighted chant of 'Off! Off! Off!', at which Coates, the gifted amateur, crossed his arms and stared at them with scorn and withering contempt.

That night the play got as far as the last act, but ended in riot when Coates suddenly re-entered with a crowbar, which was quite unnecessary and not mentioned in Shakespeare's text, to prise open the Capulets' tomb.

Of course, an actor of this calibre was soon in demand by London theatres and he arrived at the Haymarket Theatre on 9 December 1811. Here, playing Lothario in the first night of *The Fair Penitent*, Coates took longer to die on stage than anyone before or since. The audience sat politely, as his writhing figure was gripped by spasm after spasm, happy in the knowledge that it was only Act IV and that Coates would soon be dead, leaving a clear act to run without him. He died and the curtain fell.

After the interval, the gifted amateur came out before the curtain, dressed in regimental uniform, and announced that there would not be a fifth act that night. He would instead be reciting his favourite monologue.

After delighting London audiences for a further few years he retired from the stage due to bankruptcy.

The Least Successful Productions

In the closing years of the eighteenth century Mr George Frederick Cook, the actor, became too drunk to play the principal role in Charles Macklin's *Love à la Mode* at Covent Garden Theatre. This made possible one of the few occasions when a play has been performed in public without its major character.

After a brief discussion the cast decided to go along with the drama despite the absence of Sir Archy Mac-Sarcasm, the play's main wit. During the performance the heroine, Charlotte, appeared more in need of an analyst than a suitor since she seemed to be in the permanent grip of an all-embracing hysteria. In one scene she was sitting alone on the stage and had to say the following lines.

Charlotte: Ha, ha, ha!

Sir Archy: . . .

Charlotte: I beg your pardon, sir, but – ha, ha, ha, I am laughing – ha, ha, ha, to think what – ha, ha, ha.

Sir Archy: . . .

Charlotte: Ha, ha, ha! Pray, how do you make that out?

Sir Archie: . . .

Charlotte: Ha, ha, ha!

Act II contained a choice moment when the entire cast laughed ('Omnes: Ha, ha ha!') for no reason at all. It also had Mordechai embracing thin air twice and Sir Callaghan fighting the world's first unaccompanied duel. He was interrupted in this venture when Charlotte entered and said, 'Oh bless me, what are you doing?'

The same theatrical device was employed in 1787 when *Hamlet* was performed with no one playing its title role. It was to have been played at the Richmond Theatre by an inexperienced actor called Cubit who had previously been given only small walk-on parts, but he was taken unwell on the second night just before curtain-up. With Hamlet ailing in his dressing room, the manager was obliged to request that the audience 'suffer a production' that omitted him entirely.

According to Sir Walter Scott, the play was better received than on its first night, and many of the audience felt that it was an improvement on the complete play.

Most Lines Forgotten by One Actor

In one of the great stage performances of our time Mr Paul Greenwood breathed new life into a familiar old play by forgetting almost every line of his part at the Barbican Theatre, London, on 24 July 1984.

At the opening night of *The Happiest Days of Your Life* he single-handedly transformed an otherwise predictable show. The great actor strode confidently onto the stage and placed his golf bag on the table. It immediately slid off, signalling that we were in the presence of a master.

After saying a few lines correctly, perhaps to show what a dull evening it would be without his intervention, he began rummaging in his pockets so he could 'take a note' as the script demanded. It all began when his propelling pencil didn't have any lead and then his pen didn't have any ink and then he realised there was total silence on stage while he was supposed to be speaking.

Now elegantly flustered, his face was suffused with the finest expression of blankness ever seen on the London stage. He launched into a bravura selection of original lines that would have come as a great surprise to the playwright.

In Act II he varied his performance and began saying everybody else's lines, whereupon he turned to the audience and said, 'I'm sorry, I will have to stop because I'm talking nonsense here. You see, there was no lead in my pencil.' When a colleague ad-libbed that 'this has always been your problem', it brought the house down.

By Act III the excellent Mr Greenwood was completely liberated from the plot. 'Shall I start again?' he asked the enthralled audience. 'Yes,' they roared back, wishing to bask anew in such an original performance.

One theatre critic took this opportunity to review the prompter who was 'such a feature of the evening', while *The Times* hailed it as 'memory loss on a grand scale'.

The Worst Ever Variety Act

The worst act in the history of light entertainment was almost certainly the Cherry Sisters from Cedar Rapids, Iowa. Their performance was so entertaining that a wire net had to be erected across the footlights to protect them from the nightly barrage of vegetables that were regularly hurled at this unique musical quartet. The sisters themselves insisted that it was the work of envious rivals. Audiences regularly chased their bus all the way back to their hotel throwing eggs.

Their act opened with Aggie, Effie, Lizzie and Jessie walking awkwardly to the centre of the stage in shapeless, flame-red gowns, hats and woollen mittens of their own making. Three of them were tall, thin and sang, while Jessie was short, fat and played a bass drum.

They stood there acknowledging the ecstatic whoops that greeted their arrival and then launched into a uniquely strained soprano version of 'Ta-ra-ra-boom-dee-ay' that included the verse

> Cherries ripe, boom-dee-ay
> Cherries red, boom-dee-ay
> The Cherry Sisters
> Have come to stay.

The song was accompanied by a range of hearty gestures and intermittent thumps on the drum. The audience sat transfixed with disbelief until the Cherry Sisters shuffled off the stage showing not the slightest trace of nervousness or of the talent normally associated with this line of work.

In 1896 they were taken to New York by Oscar Hammerstein, the impresario, who said, 'I have tried putting on the best acts and it hasn't worked. Now I'm trying the worst.'

The *New York Times* review of their opening night on 17 November was headed 'Four Freaks from Iowa'. In it the critic said that 'all too obviously they were genuine products of the barnyard . . . Never before did New Yorkers see anything in the least like the Cherry Sisters', and suggested that their performance might be due to poor diet.

Their repertoire included 'I'm Out Upon the Mash, Boys', 'Curfew Must Not Ring Tonight', 'Don't You Remember Sweet Alice, Ben Bolt?' and 'The Modern Young Man, a Recitation'. With a growing reputation as the world's worst variety act, they played to capacity crowds all over America. Hammerstein's hunch paid off.

After a court case in 1911 the law of libel was changed to include a defence of fair comment so that theatre critics could describe the Cherry Sisters' performance without fear of litigation. You see, our sort of person has influence. We get the law changed.

The Unluckiest Stage Show

Knowing how superstitious theatre people are, Mr Lawrence Wright announced that his thirteenth production at the North Pier, Blackpool, was in fact his fourteenth. The fates now thwarted, he opened *On with the Show* in the summer of 1938.

First, the theatre burned down and all the props were destroyed. After that things began to go seriously wrong. The show was transferred to the smaller Pavilion Theatre, where Tessie O'Shea slipped, sprained her wrist and was unable to play her ukulele. Then Harry, of The Five Sherry Brothers, was rushed off with gastric troubles, an ailment also caught by the novelty vocalist, Peggy Desmond, who was out of action for a week.

Robert Naylor lost his voice, while Frank Randle had to have all his teeth pulled out and stood there in his gums for the rest of the run. Dorrane of 'Alexis and Dorrane Speciality Dancers' was ordered to take a complete rest; two members of the Health and Beauty Chorus sprained ankles, and one of the high-speed dancing Viennese Romancers fell upstairs and hurt her leg. Mr W. M. Morris, the manager, collapsed and the wardrobe mistress, Mrs E. Perry, fell and sprained her arm.

It was then discovered that there were thirteen people in the cast, thirteen musicians in the band and thirteen songs in the show.

The Worst West End Play

At the age of eighty-three the Revd Walter Reynolds wrote *Young England*, a play that received such wonderfully bad reviews that it played to full houses for 278 performances at the Victoria Palace before transferring by public demand to two other theatres in the West End of London.

Intended by its author as a serious work celebrating the triumph of good over evil and the virtues of the Boy Scout movement, it was received as an uproarious comedy.

Before long, audiences had learned the key lines and were joining in at all the choicest moments. The scout mistress rarely said the line 'I must go and attend to my girls' water' without at least fifty voices in good-humoured support.

The plot, which was never cheapened by a sense of humour, tells of a Major Carlingford, a betrayer of women, shady promoter and sanctimonious humbug, who spent the greater part of the evening conspiring with his scoundrel son to ruin a popular and heroic young man who is not only a scoutmaster, a town councillor and a parliamentary candidate, but also a talented engineer destined to improve the appearance of the River Thames at Charing Cross.

When the play opened in September 1934, the *Daily Telegraph*'s critic wrote:

> The villain makes plain his felony by constantly wearing a top hat in the depths of the country. His son, 'the second robber', is some sort of officer in the boy scouts and brings shame upon that highly respected body by committing his major crime while dressed in his uniform. But he at least has the grace to get into immaculate evening dress proper to his kind when he wants to get drunk.

The show went from strength to strength, even though its clergyman author periodically roamed the aisles remonstrating with hecklers and shaking his fists.

The Least Informative Book

During 1944 Mr Keith Odo Newman wrote a book entitled *250 Times I Saw a Play*. It is an account of his visits to every performance of the same stage show, including matinees. The charm of the book lies in the fact that, while he wishes to give us a complete understanding of this experience, he nowhere tells us what the play was, who wrote it, where it was performed or who acted in it.

Although he proudly announces that he himself thought up the title of the play, he still cannot be tempted to share it with us. Instead he writes at great length on the subject of sadomasochism. 'It may well be asked by the reader how this discourse about sadism and masochism is relevant to the study. I believe it is,' he writes. Happily, he does not attempt to say why it is relevant, but restricts himself to giving us a potted biography of the Marquis de Sade.

In the chapter on 'Impersonation' he considers at some length the difference between acting and impersonating. The next chapter is entitled 'Back to the Play', but rather cleverly he does not go back to the play at all. Instead he continues with his views on impersonation. The book ends with his guess that the mental age of the average audience is around sixteen.

Asked for his comments, George Bernard Shaw replied, 'I don't know what to say about this book', a tribute that was cheerfully printed on its cover.

The Worst Playwright

This honour falls to Mr Edward Falconer. His interminable prose style reached astonishing new heights with the production on 19 November 1866 of *Oonagh* or *The Lovers of Lismona*. In it Falconer attempted to merge the stories of two quite separate novels, both fairly long in their original form.

The play started at 7.30 p.m. and went on, and on, and on. At 11 p.m., lulled by the finest platitudes, the audience slumbered. Midnight came and the play meandered on its way. According to the critics, the 'audience folded their tents and stole silently away like Arabs', while the cast continued relentlessly onwards.

By 2 a.m. only a handful of critics and Bohemians remained, slumped in bored slumber. With 3 a.m. looming, the stagehands held a meeting and voted to take the law into their own hands. For the sake of everyone involved, they lowered the curtain. *Oonagh* was silenced. It did not have a second night.

The Most Embarrassed Author

Charles Lamb set a fine example on December 1806 when he booed the premiere of his own play, *Mr H*. Although he had packed the Drury Lane Theatre with his closest friends, they could not tolerate the work and nor, it turned out, could the author. It purported to be a farce but its only humour centred on the protagonist being called 'Hogsflesh'.

When a few gentle boos emanated from the stalls these were soon multiplied by Lamb himself from his seat in the front row. The critic Crabb Robinson recollected that Lamb 'was probably the loudest hisser in the house'.

Afterwards, the author said he absolutely agreed with the audience's verdict and started hissing so they would not think he had written it. The management wanted to let the play run, but the playwright begged them to take it off.

The Shortest West End Run

The shortest West End run was of a play called *The Lady of Lyons* by Lord Lytton. It opened on 26 December 1888 at the Shaftesbury Theatre. After waiting patiently for an hour, the audience was dismissed because no one could open the safety curtain.

10

MEDIA STUDIES

The Least Accurate Newspaper Report
The Worst Broadcast
The Most Unsuccessful TV Commercial
The Least Successful Newspaper
The Least Successful Newshound
The Most Pointless Radio Interview
The Least Successful Sound Effect
The Least Successful Weather Forecast
The Longest Errata List
The Least Successful Newspaper Competition
The Most Misprints in a Newspaper
The Least Interesting Live TV Show
The Least Popular TV Programme
The Least Successful New Year Broadcast

'It was I myself who personally and accidentally
goofed.'
DAVID OGILVY

The Least Accurate Newspaper Report

Newspaper reporters make mistakes, of course, but few have been more innovative than one who contributed a personality profile of a local man called 'Harris' to the *Wiltshire Times and Chippenham News* in 1963. The following week the paper carried a magnificent apology.

Mr Harris, it said, has asked us to point out a number of inaccuracies in our story. After returning from India, he served in Ireland for four years and not six months as stated; he never farmed at Heddington, particularly not at Coate Road Farm as stated; he has never counted cycling or walking among his hobbies; he is not a member of fifty-four hunts, and he did not have an eye removed at Chippenham Hospital after an air raid on Calne.

'My only disappointment when interviewing him,' wrote the reporter in his original article, 'was that I could not spare more time with this raconteur.'

The Worst Broadcast

Few broadcasters have given more unalloyed pleasure than Lieutenant Commander Tommy Woodroofe. He leaped to public prominence with his now famous commentary on the illumination of the fleet at Spithead in 1937.

Before the broadcast the Commander had joined in celebrations with slightly too much enthusiasm. The result was an exquisitely incoherent talk punctuated by pauses of anything up to eleven seconds.

'At the present moment,' he began, 'the whole fleet is lit up. When I say "lit up" I mean lit up by fairy lamps. It's fantastic. It isn't a fleet at all. It's just . . . It's fairyland. The whole fleet is in fairyland. Now if you'll follow me through . . . If you don't mind . . . The next few moments you'll find the fleet doing odd things.'

There then followed a lengthy pause. 'I'm sorry. I was telling some people to shut up talking,' the Commander explained delightfully.

At this point all the lights on the fleet were turned out so that rockets could be fired. The Commander's reaction was: 'It's gone. It's gone. There's no fleet. It's . . . It's disappeared. No magician whoever could have waved his wand could have waved it with more acumen than he has now at the present moment. The fleet's gone . . . It's disappeared. I was talking to you in the middle of this damn . . . (*coughs*) in the middle of this fleet and what's happened is the fleet's gone and disappeared and gone.'

At this point Commander Woodroofe was faded out; an announcer said, 'That is the end of the Spithead commentary', and dance music came on.

Commander Woodroofe said afterwards that he had been 'overcome by emotion'.

The Most Unsuccessful TV Commercial

The comedian Pat Coombs is the proud holder of the record for the largest number of unsuccessful 'takes' for a television commercial. In 1973, while making a breakfast cereal advertisement, she forgot her lines twenty-eight times. On each occasion she forgot the same thing – the name of the product.

When asked five years later what the product was, she replied, 'I still can't remember. It was some sort of muesli, but the name was practically unpronounceable. They were very kind to me, but that only made it worse. I had total stage fright every time the camera came near me. With each take I got worse. It's put me off cereal for life.'

The commercial was never finished and the product was taken off the market soon afterwards.

The Least Successful Newspaper

Described on billboards as 'Britain's most fearless newspaper', the *Commonwealth Sentinel* opened on 6 February 1965 and closed on the 7th. Designed to cater for all Commonwealth citizens, the paper was founded by Mr Lionel Burleigh in London. He spent a hectic week collecting the advertisements, writing the stories and seeing the first issue through the press. Then Mr Burleigh received a phone call from the police.

'Are you anything to do with the *Commonwealth Sentinel?*' asked a constable, encouraged by a hysterical hotel porter. 'Because there are fifty thousand of them out-side the entrance to Brown's Hotel and they're blocking Albemarle Street.'

'We had forgotten to arrange any distribution,' Mr Burleigh said later, 'and they were just dumped outside the hotel where I was staying. To my knowledge we only sold one copy. I still have the money in my drawer.' It was sold by Mr Burleigh's daughter to a passer-by. This caused so much excitement that a photograph was tak-en of the transaction.

The Least Successful Newshound

V. S. Pritchett was a celebrated literary critic, but we can overlook this in view of his contribution to hard news reporting.

In the 1920s he took a job as a reporter on the *Christian Science Monitor*.

Long after the event he said about his time as the *Monitor*'s correspondent in Northern Ireland, 'I simply didn't know what news was. I missed every important occasion. Even now I don't know what news is.'

He once missed the resignation of a cabinet minis-ter because he 'couldn't see how it mattered'. His fin-est achievement came in 1922 when he was sent to cover the war in Spanish Morocco. 'Any enterprising reporter would have gone into the hills to interview the Moroccan leader Abdul Krin, but not me. The idea filled me with horror and I vigorously abstained. All I heard was a lot of gunfire in the evenings,' he said. 'But it was a lovely country.'

The Most Pointless Radio Interview

One of Britain's most popular radio programmes is *Desert Island Discs*, in which a celebrity is asked to imagine that, for unspecified reasons, he is trapped on a desert island with his eight favourite musical recordings.

In the early 1970s the programme's presenter, Roy Plomley, was keen to get the novelist Alistair Maclean onto the show. As a writer of adventure stories, it was felt he might fit the role of a castaway and give a gripping broadcast.

This was soon arranged despite Maclean's known reluctance to give interviews.

Mr Plomley went to meet him for lunch at the Savile Club in London. They got on extremely well.

During lunch Mr Plomley asked, 'Which part of the year do you put aside for your writing?'

'Writing?' said Maclean.

'Yes – your books – *Guns of Navarone*.'

'I'm not Alistair Maclean, the writer.'

'No?'

'No. I'm in charge of the Ontario Tourist Bureau.'

With no alternative, the two set off of the studio. During the recording an increasingly agitated producer urged, 'Ask him about his books.'

'He hasn't written any,' replied the interviewer.

The programme was never broadcast.

The Least Successful Sound Effect

In 1944 King Haakon of Norway delivered a rousing wartime address to his beleaguered people on the BBC World Service. As his Royal Highness was running forty seconds short, the producer sent to the library for a fanfare to round things off. At this point the talk came brilliantly alive.

Haakon had just commended his country to God, made a few Nordic farewell grunts and laid down his script, when the air was suddenly alive with the sound of roundabouts and ribaldry and cockneys shouting, 'Roll up, roll up, ladies and gentlemen.' The library had sent a funfair. Afterwards the King said it was 'the sort of thing that happens'.

The Least Successful Weather Forecast

At the end of a bravura weather forecast in October 1987 Mr Michael Fish told British televiewers that 'a woman rang to say she'd heard there was a hurricane on the way. Well, don't worry. There isn't.' Brushing aside this fanciful amateur forecast with a chuckle, the immortal Fish predicted 'sea breezes' and a 'showery airflow'.

In no time Britain was hit by 120 mph winds that ripped up three hundred miles of power cables, plunged a quarter of the country into darkness, blocked two hundred roads with fallen branches, felled 25 per cent of the trees in Kent and stopped all rail traffic in the south of England for twenty-four hours. An ambulance at Hayling Island was hit by yacht floating across the road and the Meteorological Office said it was the worst since 1703.

A spokesman for Mr Fish later said, 'It is really all a question of detail.'

The Longest Errata List

A booklet entitled *The History of Cornish Pubs* gained extreme popularity in 1978 on account of its impressive errata list.

It contained 140 corrections to a 70-page survey. High spots include:

page 3, line 1: for 'assuming' read 'unassuming'
page 8, line 54: for 'White Hart' read 'White Horse'
page 13, line 49: for 'major' read 'minor'
page 32, line 19: for 'Mews' read 'mess'
page 33, line 44: for 'Bishop and Wool' read 'Bridge on Wool'
page 63, line 6: for 'Queen's Arms' read 'Queen's Head'
page 73, line 5: for 'ship' read 'moulded ceilings'
page 73, line 6: for 'Batallick' read 'Botallack' and for 'Bosliwick' read 'Boslowick'

In the book, which is subtitled 'Pubs with a storey to tell', the engagingly modest editor says, 'We must apologise for the minor mistakes which have cropped up between correcting the proof and printing. Some are my fault, others, like a car one takes in to have repaired, the fault is repaired, but others occur! A few we have not corrected, especially punctuations! It should be possible to insert these in the text.'

The Least Successful Newspaper Competition

In May 1986 the distinguished British journalist Henry Porter revealed that he had planted five deliberate grammatical errors in his *Sunday Times* column and would send a bottle of champagne to any reader who spotted them all correctly.

Letters poured in by the sackload. The next week Mr Porter announced that readers had not found one of his five mistakes. However, they had located a further twenty-three of which he was not aware.

This overtakes the previous best. In 1964 the *Carmel Independent* in California printed a school photograph and asked readers to identify which child became a well-known celebrity. While cropping the picture for publication, an enthusiastic sub-editor cut out the child in question, making it impossible to win the contest from merely looking at the paper.

The Most Misprints in a Newspaper

The Times goes from strength to strength. On 15 March 1978 it achieved an impressive seventy-eight misprints in one page. Among the news items covered were 'Sir Harold Wilson's action in making public an 'oss.'

Further extending the freedom of the press some three months later, they carried an astonishing ninety-seven errors in only five and a half inches of one story. It concerned Pope Paul VI, who was referred to through-out as 'the Pop', and dwelt on his 'swping rorganization' of the papal curia.

It said that: 'Th Scrtariat of Stat, the vatican's fori-gnoffic, gratly expand, its activities as Pop Paul pushed normalization of church relations with communist and other countris.' Furthermore, 'Incrased collegiality in th running of th church ld to cration of the synod of Bish-ops, a large gathering of ky bishops vtry thre yars and an organisation to maintain these contacts in between synods.'

In an age when many feel that modern popes have become a shade too populist, this fascinating report does much to restore to the papacy some of its lost mystery.

The Least Interesting Live TV Show

In April 1986 the WGN TV station got a scoop. Amid much ballyhoo they announced they were going to unseal Al Capone's secret vault beneath the Lexington

Hotel, Chicago. It was said to contain a hoard of missing money, diamonds, whiskey and the bones of those who had 'upset' him.

Entitled *The Mystery of Al Capone's Vaults*, the two-hour live show was hosted by an excited reporter who wore an excavation helmet and a large moustache. 'I am Geraldo Rivera and you're about to witness a live television event,' he gasped. 'Now for the first time that vault is going to be opened live. This is an adventure you and I will take together.'

The show was syndicated across the whole of America and there was a carnival-like atmosphere with hundreds celebrating at an 'Al Capone Safe-Cracking Charity Ball'. Also in attendance was a small army of law enforcement officials, reporters, Internal Revenue agents, employees of the Federal Treasury, claiming that Capone still owed them $800,000, and criminal technicians who were there gathering evidence.

To add an air of authenticity to the production, Rivera demonstrated the use of a prohibition-era Thompson sub-machine gun and detonated a dynamite blast using a Capone-style plunger.

Tension mounted as an explosives team arrived. After an hour and a half blasting through the walls the dust settled and the cameras went in, accompanied by Dr Robert Stein, the County Medical Examiner, who was on hand in case bones or mummified bodies were found.

The vault contains two empty gin bottles and Geraldo filled in the time by singing 'Chicago'.

The Least Popular TV Programme

In 1978 an opinion poll showed that a French television programme was watched by no viewers at all.

The great day for French broadcasting was 14 August, when not one person saw an extensive interview with an Armenian woman on her fortieth birthday. It ranged over the way she met her husband, her illnesses and the joy of living.

The poll said that 67 per cent had preferred a Napoleonic costume drama and 33 per cent had opted for *It's a Knockout*.

The programme was transmitted at peak-viewing time and was selected in the previous day's *France-Soir* as the best programme on the channel that evening.

The Least Successful New Year Broadcast

The world watched with growing admiration as Chancellor Helmut Kohl of West Germany steamed ahead with pioneering work in this field. In 1987 national TV got the wrong tape and re-ran the speech he had given the year before. Everyone was enchanted to hear it again.

On 1 January 1988 all Germany gathered round their TV sets to see if it would be shown for a record-breaking third time. But that year things went even better. First, it was wrongly introduced as 'The Chancellor's Christmas Message', whereupon the screen went blank for two minutes. When the presenter came back to correct this error, he impressed the entire nation by announcing a completely different programme. 'And now,' he said, '*Dinner for One*, Freddie Frinton's comedy sketch about an overworked butler.'

At this point Chancellor Kohl appeared and started talking about the economy.

11

LAW AND ORDER

The Worst Burglar
The Worst Bank Robbers
The Worst Moment for a Crime
The Least Successful Attempt to Catch a Thief
The Least Successful Act of Public Bravery
The Crimes That Were Easiest to Detect
The Least Successful Secret Camera
The Worst Jury
The Most Unsuccessful Prison Escape
The Least Successful Getaways
The Gang Who Got Lost
The Least Successful Safe Breakers
The Least Successful Jewellery Raid
The Least Successful Car Theft
The Least Successful Armed Robbery
The Most Ignored Robber
The Danish Dimension, Part One
The Danish Dimension, Part Two
Burgling the Wrong Place
Stealing the Wrong Thing
Crime Busters
The Least Successful Safe Motoring Competition

The Most Pointless Bank Raid
The Possibilities of Marble
Prompt Police Action
The Least Alert Burglar

'They say best men are moulded out of faults
And, for the most, become much more better
For being a little bad.'
WILLIAM SHAKESPEARE, *Measure for Measure*, V:1

The Worst Burglar

The history of crime offers few figures less suited to undetected burglary than Mr Philip McCutcheon.

He was arrested for the twentieth time when, after his latest robbery, he drove his getaway car into two parked vans. During his appearance at York Crown Court in 1971, the judge gave a rare display of careers advice from the bench.

Giving our man a conditional discharge, Mr Rodney Percy, the Recorder said, 'I think you should give burglary up. You have a withered hand, an artificial leg and only one eye. You have been caught in Otley, Leeds, Harrogate, Norwich, Beverley, Howell and York. How can you hope to succeed?

'You are a rotten burglar. You are always being caught.'

The Worst Bank Robbers

In August 1975 three men were on their way in to rob the Royal Bank of Scotland at Rothesay, when they got stuck in the revolving doors. They had to be helped free by the staff and, after thanking everyone, sheepishly left the building.

A few minutes later they returned and announced their intention of robbing the bank, but none of the staff believed them. When, at first, they demanded £5,000 the head cashier laughed at them, convinced that it was a practical joke.

Considerably disheartened by this, the gang leader reduced his demand first to £500, then to £50 and ultimately to 50 pence. By this stage the cashier could barely control herself for laughter.

Then one of the men jumped over the counter and fell awkwardly on the floor, clutching his ankle. The other two made their getaway, but got trapped in the revolving doors for a second time, desperately pushing the wrong way.

The Worst Moment for a Crime

Choosing the right moment is vitally important in any crime. Mr David Goodall of Barnsley, for example, set off in January 1979 to do a bit of shoplifting. Once inside the Barnsley branch of British Home Stores he had hardly stolen his first item when he was simultaneously seized by eight pairs of hands. The shop was holding a convention of store detectives at the time.

The Least Successful Attempt to
Catch a Thief

During 1978 a persistent thief had stolen £10 nightly from a newsagent's shop in Barking, Essex. Every morning cash was missing from the till and so the shopkeeper devised a plan to catch the culprit.

Into his shop the owner transported a giant cardboard box which he placed unostentatiously in the middle of the floor. After five o'clock closing, he climbed into the box wherein he spent the entire night.

Nothing stirred until fourteen hours later when the excellent sleuth, tired and stiff, emerged at dawn to answer a call of nature. Minutes later he returned, stretching a leg here and rubbing a neck there, to discover that, in his absence, the thief had been, taken £10 from the till and gone again.

The Least Successful Act of Public Bravery

Occasionally a member of the public steps in bravely to prevent crime. In July 1978 bank employees at Sherman Oaks in California thought they had outwitted a robber when they refused to handle a suspicious package.

Relieved staff watched as the bandit sprinted out of the bank to dump his parcel. However, a man standing outside the bank saw the robber escaping and chased after him. He tackled the thief and returned the package, which, in fact, contained tear gas timed to explode in two minutes, to the bank. It took thirty minutes to clear the air.

The Crimes That Were Easiest to Detect

Any act of genius is marked by a dazzling simplicity. There is about it a logic and inevitability that is deeply satisfying. The following crimes were detected almost immediately.

In 1972 Mr J. Egan from London stole a barge on the River Thames and was very soon caught. There was a dock strike on and his was the only craft moving that day.

Mr J. Ealey committed a burglary in Detroit in 1968 and left his dog at the scene of the crime. The police soon arrived and shouted, 'Home, boy.' They then followed the dog back to the burglar's house and arrived only seconds after he did.

In May 1976 Vernon Drinkwater and Raymond Heap of Blackburn were accused of stealing a car while trying to sell it to its original owner.

In 1978 Allan Bonds and Bernard Redfearn of Stoke-on-Trent stole a water tank, but forgot that it was still half full. They left a trail of puddles and got home minutes before the police.

All the above, however, are entirely eclipsed by Mr Clive Bunyan who raided the village store at Cayton, Yorkshire, in 1970, wearing a crash helmet with the words 'clive bunyan' written in large gold letters across the front – a definitive performance.

The Least Successful Secret Camera

Attempting to catch a persistent thief in 1978, the Doncaster police set up a secret camera in the changing rooms of a local squash club.

When they played back the film, the police found that all they had succeeded in filming was one of their own policeman wandering round naked and looking for his clothes, which had been stolen.

The Worst Jury

A murder trial at Manitoba in February 1978 was well advanced when one juror revealed that he was completely deaf and did not have the remotest clue what was happening.

The judge, Mr Justice Solomon, asked him if he had heard any evidence at all and, when there was no reply, dismissed him.

The excitement this caused was equalled only when a second juror revealed that he spoke not a word of English. A fluent French speaker, he exhibited great surprise when told, after two days, that he was hearing a murder trial.

The trial was abandoned when a third juror said that he suffered from both conditions, being simultaneously unversed in the English language and nearly as deaf as the first juror.

The judge ordered a retrial.

The Most Unsuccessful Prison Escape

After weeks of extremely careful planning, seventy-five convicts completely failed to escape from Saltillo Prison in northern Mexico. In November 1975 they had started digging a secret tunnel designed to bring them up at the other side of the prison wall.

On 18 April 1976, guided by pure genius, their tunnel came up in the nearby courtroom in which many of them had been sentenced. The surprised judges returned all seventy-five to jail.

The Least Successful Getaways

A bank robber in Malta set a new world best when he raided the Bank of Valetta, held up the staff, seized the cash, rushed out, dashed across the road and waited at the bus stop. After fifteen minutes, with no bus in sight, he was arrested by a passing policeman whose suspicions were aroused by the three thousand new banknotes he was clasping to his chest.

And in 1976 Mr Alfred Riviera showed the importance of split-second timing. After he had robbed a bar in San Fernando he dashed out and sprinted down the road to a prearranged meeting place where he was knocked over by his own getaway car.

The Gang Who Got Lost

At 5 a.m. on September 1981 the Edmonton Two raided the Petro-Canada fuel station in Vancouver, locked the attendant in the washroom and made their getaway with one hundred dollars. Coming from Edmonton, they did not know their way around Vancouver and twenty minutes later they drove up at the same petrol station to ask for directions.

The attendant, Mr Karnail Dhillon, had just escaped from the washroom and so was alarmed to see the burly pair approaching the cashier's window again. 'They wanted me to tell them the way to Port Moody,' he said. 'I guess they didn't recognise me or the station.'

He was just calling the police when the pair came back yet again to say they could not get their car started. They were on the phone to a towing company when they were arrested by Police Constable Tom Dreschel.

The Least Successful Safe-Breakers

Using the latest sophisticated equipment, a gang from Chichester set about cutting open a safe at the Southern Leisure Centre. Happily, it was the wrong sophisticated equipment and in no time they had welded up the door. The manager said that after their good work the safe was so secure that it took three hours to open using a hammer and chisel.

The Least Successful Jewellery Raid

With a thoughtfulness that is rare nowadays, Paul Lassis alerted the staff of a Bristol jewellery shop to his forthcoming raid by sounding his car horns loudly, while driving up on the pavement outside.

With the entire staff watching, he reached out to smash the shop window. As his hammer bounced harmlessly off the toughened glass, he tried to reverse his car through it, but missed, crashed over a wastepaper bin and was stuck fast when a passing evangelical missionary, Mr Herbert Eaton, prevented a getaway by hurling his bicycle through the car's windscreen.

The Least Successful Car Theft

While parked in 1987 outside the garage of Mr Colin Baggs, a suspected car thief, two policemen had allowed their windows to steam up. Having gained no evidence whatsoever to support their case, they were just on the point of giving up when Mr Baggs broke into their vehicle.

The immortal Baggs was himself unable to explain this moment of brilliance, but admiring members of Frome magistrates' bench described it as 'a classic own goal'.

The Least Successful Armed Robbery

Few armed robbers have taken a more original approach to their calling than the innovator who held up Mohammed Razaq's grocery store in Wandsworth on 20 July 1979. Bursting in from Felsham Road, he said, 'Give me the money from your till or I will shoot.'

Even in moments of high drama Mr Razaq prides himself on his eye for detail. 'Where is your gun?' he asked. At this point the great innovator had to reply that he didn't actually have a gun, but if there were any further difficulties he would go out, get one and come back. Having made this point, he left.

The Most Ignored Robber

In February 1986 Mr David Morris of West Croydon devised a foolproof scheme to get rich quick without saying a word. All he would have to do was to march into any local shop and hold up a fearsome sheet of paper bearing the message: 'I have a gun in my pocket. I will shoot if you do not hand over the money.'

Putting this to the test, he went into the chemist's. The female assistant thought it was an obscene note and refused to read it. At the Asian delicatessen next door the owner gazed blankly at the words, shook his head and said he could not read English. And at the Chinese takeaway the manager announced that he did not have his glasses. It was while supposedly searching for them in the back room that he called the police who put an end to what could have been an extremely promising career.

The Danish Dimension, Part One

In June 1987 three enterprising Danish robbers worked long and hard, trying to dynamite open a safe at the bank in Munkebo, Denmark. Despite detonating six times the required amount of dynamite, they found that the safe remained firmly closed. They did, however, demolish the bank and the explosion was reported ten miles away.

The Danish Dimension, Part Two

Racing out of a Copenhagen bank in 1978, a Danish thief flagged down a police car. Thinking it was a taxi because it had a light on top, he jumped in the back with a sack full of money and shouted out his home address.

When the bank manager rushed out seeking a policeman to catch this thief, his task could not have been easier.

Burgling the Wrong Place

Under cover of night Vincent Pattison rowed across Regent's Canal in London and broke into the wrong warehouse. Anyone could have done this; it required no skill. However, faced with this situation, a duller man might have gone outside and broken into the correct building.

Not so Mr Pattison who inexplicably started sledge-hammering through the wall. Who knows how this promising crime might have developed had not a police car drawn up outside to investigate the impressive din?

Giving up all hope of total demolition, our hero jumped back onto his boat, whereupon it sank and he had to swim to the opposite shore and hide in a nearby block of flats. The police chased ended when Mr Pattison sneezed.

Stealing the Wrong Thing

With a daring that many of their older colleagues could hardly equal, two teenagers broke into a Yeovil grocery shop in April 1984.

Messrs Knibbs and Hunt located what they thought was the cash box, wrenched it from the wall and escaped into the street. When the box started up a shrill buzzing, they threw it to the ground and stamped on it, but to no avail. Despite all their efforts to stop the noise this enter-prising duo finally had to dump the box in the river. They had stolen the burglar alarm.

Crime Busters

In July 1985 four West London criminals made extensive plans to rob the manager of the White Knight Laundry in Kensal Road as he left the bank with a box full of staff wages. The police were, however, tipped off and they too made extensive plans to catch them in the act.

Both parties, police and criminals, were stationed outside Barclays Bank in Chamberlayne Road, Kensal Rise, and the manager was inside with a specially emptied box. As he stepped through the door, everybody was just about to act when another thief dashed out from a doorway, snatched the empty box and disappeared without trace.

The Least Successful Safe Motoring Competition

Wishing to enhance their country's reputation for careful driving, the French police held a safe motoring contest in 1987. The plan was to award free petrol tokens to motorists who impressed roadside police with their respect for the law and concern for others.

After several days they had still not awarded a single prize and so the police decided to lower their standards. Thereafter they would give the tokens to any driver who was obeying the basic traffic regulations. Even this proved difficult.

When gendarmes tried to flag down the first winner, he assumed he was in trouble and raced away. When they signalled for the second winner to pull off the road, he accelerated through a red traffic light and the police had to book him instead.

In the end they gave the award to anyone they could find with a current driving licence whose car was fitted with a seatbelt.

The Most Pointless Bank Raid

With split-second timing and consummate teamwork four masked men raided a bank at Artema near Rome in February 1980. Not knowing that the bank had closed three minutes early 'because things were quiet', the gang's leader ran headlong into a locked plate-glass door and knocked himself out.

Falling back into the arms of three accomplices, he was carried to the waiting getaway car and driven off. According to bank officials, this complex raid was completed in just under four minutes.

The Possibilities of Marble

Marble floors offer unique opportunities to the Italian bank robber and Carlo Colodi has explored many of them. In September 1979 he parked his car outside Milan's Banca Agricultura and dashed in with a scarf hiding his face and a revolver in his hand.

Hitting his foot on the corner of the mat, he slid across the marble floor. His scarf dropped off, revealing his face, and, as he fell, he accidentally fired his revolver. Scrambling hastily to his feet, he ran to the cashier's desk, skidded wildly and grabbed at a counter to keep his balance. To do this he had to drop the gun, where-upon, according to one newspaper report, 'the entire bank rocked with hilarity'.

Rightly offended by this lack of appreciation, our man ceased his artistry, turned, ran, slipped and crawled out of the bank to find a police officer writing out a ticket for his car, which was parked in a no-waiting zone.

Prompt Police Action

West Midlands police moved swiftly on 15 May 1983 when a caller rang to say there was an abandoned safe on a grass verge at Halesowen. In no time a uniformed officer was on the scene, where he stood guard for over an hour until the arrival of detectives who dusted it for fingerprints.

This important work done, they tried taking the safe back to the police station. When all attempts at lifting it failed, the uniformed branch sent a team of constables to help, but even they could not budge it so the traffic division sent a Land Rover with towing gear. Man and machine united for twenty minutes of fruitless constabulary shoving.

'That', said an officer, 'was when we realised it was a Midlands Electricity Board junction box concreted into the ground.'

The Least Alert Burglar

A Parisian villain broke into a house at the village of Lachelle in 1964. Once inside he began to feel decidedly peckish and so went in search of the refrigerator. There he found his favourite cheese, which it would have been a shame not to try.

He then found some Bath Oliver biscuits and three bottles of champagne.

After a while he began to feel sleepy and decided that he would lie down and digest his meal in comfort. He was arrested next morning fast asleep upstairs in the spare bedroom.

12

LOVE AND MARRIAGE

The Least Whirlwind Romance
The Least Successful Latin Lover
The Burglar Who Fell in Love with His Victim
The Least Successful Date
The Least Successful Embrace
The Least Successful Pornographic Bookseller
The Most Unsuccessful Attempt to Die for Love
The Least Successful Abduction
The Shortest Period of Marital Bliss
The Brides Who Married the Wrong Grooms
The Most Divorces from the Same Person
The Least Successful Alibi

'If anything can go wrong it will.'
MURPHY'S LAW

The Least Whirlwind Romance

In 1900 Octavio Guillen met the girl who would one day be his wife. Two years later he announced his engagement to Adriana Martinez and everyone said they made a lovely couple.

They still made a lovely couple in 1969, when they cast caution to the wind and got married in Mexico City. They were both eighty-two and had been engaged for sixty-seven years.

The Least Successful Latin Lover

In 1977 Signor Paco Vila, a student from Palermo in Italy, was carried out on a stretcher, after having his cheek caressed in a discothèque.

In many respects Signor Vila had the mainstream Latin interests and approach. 'I am mad about big English-women,' he said, after regaining consciousness in a hospital bed. 'But they scorn me because I lack the weight.'

He was on the skinny side and, in a valiant effort to offset this, he started wearing thick woolly jumpers beneath a shirt.

At this particular discothèque he had so disguised his problem that he succeeded in getting an English girl on holiday at Palermo to dance with him.

During one of his more frisky rumbas he used so much energy that, when the girl boldly stroked his cheek, he collapsed in a dead faint. When examined later by doctors, he was found to be wearing seventeen woolly sweaters under his shirt and to weigh only seven stone.

The Burglar Who Fell in Love with His Victim

One of the great romantic encounters occurred in November 1978 between a Streatham burglar and the blonde into whose house he had broken.

As soon as he saw the lady he changed his tack entirely, choosing this, of all unlikely moments, to woo her.

After thirty minutes he was getting on so famously that he tried to kiss her. To his horror, she not only refused, but also felled him with a right-hand punch, a left-hand jab and a half nelson.

In this state she frogmarched him to the porter's lodge, while hitting him on the head with a spare shoe.

'She was no ordinary helpless female,' the burglar commented, on discovering that prior to a sex change she had been employed as a bricklayer.

The Least Successful Date

In the spring of 1978 Mr Tom Horsley, a thirty-year-old accountant from San Jose, invited Miss Alyn

Chesselet out for the evening. At the very last minute she cancelled.

Mr Horsley then sued her.

He went to the San Francisco Small Claims Court and filed a suit against Miss Chesselet on the grounds that she had 'broken an oral contract to have dinner and see the musical *The Wiz*'.

Mr Horsley, who made a hundred-mile round trip to visit her, informed the court that he wanted to be paid for two hours of driving to and from San Francisco at his minimum rate of £4.70 an hour as a certified public accountant plus 9.40p a mile in car expenses. His claim was for £18.80 plus a £1.10 filing fee and £1.10 to serve court papers – a total of £21.

When the court notified Miss Chesselet, a thirty-year-old waitress at the Vasuvio café in San Francisco, she said that Mr Horsley was 'nuts'.

The Least Successful Embrace

In 1976 Dr Brian Richards of Deal in Kent discovered one of the great love stories of all time, while in Regent's Park, London.

He came across a semi-clad gentleman who had slipped a disc while enjoying himself in the back of a sports car with his girlfriend.

Since the man was transfixed with agony, his girlfriend was unable to get out for help. In desperation she jammed her foot against the horn.

This attracted Dr Richards, an ambulance man, a fireman and a large crowd of passers-by who formed a circle around the car. 'You'll never get them out of there,' said the fireman, who then set about cutting the back off the car.

Trained for desperate situations, two women voluntary workers arrived and began serving hot sweet tea through the window. 'It was like the Blitz,' one of them commented.

Eventually, the lover was carried off in agony. Ambulancemen told the girlfriend that his recovery prospects were good. 'Sod him,' she replied. 'What is worrying me is how I shall explain to my husband what's happened to his car.'

The Least Successful Pornographic Bookseller

In February 1970 a Swiss pornographic bookseller was fined the equivalent of £47 and given a ten-month suspended sentence because his books were not sufficiently pornographic.

Angry residents of Biel took him to court because his wares were not as 'sexually erotic' as his advertising campaign had led them to believe. At the hearing many of them expressed the view that had they been interested in veils, curtains, cushions and household plants they would have bought a furniture catalogue.

The Most Unsuccessful Attempt to Die for Love

When his fiancée broke off their engagement in 1978, Señor Abel Ruiz of Madrid decided to kill himself for love. Reviewing the possibilities available on such occasions, he opted to prostrate himself before the Gerona-to-Madrid express. However, jumping in its path he landed between the rails and watched as the train passed safely over him. He suffered only minor injuries and promptly received first aid at Gerona Hospital.

Later that day Señor Ruiz tried again. This time he jumped in front of a passing lorry, but only acquired some more bruises. His rapid return to the hospital led doctors to call a priest, who made him see the folly of his acts. Eventually he decided to carry on living and look for a new girlfriend. Glad to be alive, he left the hospital and was knocked down by a runaway horse. He was taken back to Gerona Hospital for the third time that day, seriously injured this time.

The Least Successful Abduction

In August 1972 Mr Darsun Yilmaz of Damali on the Black Sea was spurned by his neighbour's daughter and decided to abduct her. Soon after midnight the intrepid Yilmaz arrived in his beloved's garden with a ladder. Once in her room, he threw a blanket over her head and carried her down to the car, whispering torrid endearments into that end of the blanket where one might reasonably expect her ear to be.

Away they sped into the night, joy in his heart and stars in the sky. However, when he unwrapped his precious cargo and pursed his lips for a kiss he discovered to his astonishment that it was the girl's ninety-one-year-old granny, who took this welcome opportunity to beat him up.

The Shortest Period of Marital Bliss

Jerzy and Kathryn Sluckin got married at Kensington Register Office in November 1975. Within an hour of the wedding Kathryn surprised her husband and relatives when she announced at the reception, 'It won't work', and vanished. Her husband later heard that his wife was living in a Divine Light Meditation Commune in Finchley.

'I had a few doubts before the wedding,' she admitted afterwards, 'but didn't want to say anything.'

The Brides Who Married the Wrong Grooms

At a Muslim double wedding in Jeddah a Saudi Arabian father gave his two veiled daughters away to the wrong grooms. During the ceremony in December 1978 he accomplished a slip of the tongue when he announced his approval of the marriages to the registrar and confused the names of the brides and grooms. A few days after the ceremony, the girls told their father that divorce would be unnecessary since they were quite satisfied with their husbands.

'It happens all the time,' a guest explained.

The Most Divorces from the Same Person

In January 1970 Dorothy and David King Funk obtained their fifth divorce from one another.

The complaint for divorce in this last case was filed by Mrs Funk seven months after their fifth wedding ceremony.

The couple first married in December 1950 and this lasted seven years. There were also divorced in 1962, 1964 and 1965. On each occasion the marriage was ruled to have broken down irreparably.

The Least Successful Alibi

During his divorce hearing in July 1978, a London window cleaner was asked to explain what he and 'the other woman' were doing in his bedroom with the lights out. He replied, 'Playing snooker.'

The judge, Aubrey Myerson QC, said, 'To my mind it is rather difficult to play a game of snooker in a room where the lights are off.'

He was next asked to explain the noises of passionate abandon which his wife heard coming from the house.

He replied that it was 'an expression of surprise or dis-appointment made when playing a difficult shot'.

Then he was asked why, on another occasion, 'the other woman' had been seen without her trousers on. His explanation was that she 'was doing some sewing and altering her slacks'.

His wife did not believe it and nor did the judge.

🖝 13 🖜

THE BRITISH WAY OF
DOING THINGS

The Least Successful Club
The Least Correct Astrologer
The Least Accurate Index
The Least Successful Tourist Resort
The Not Terribly Good Samaritan
The Least Successful Men's Rights Group
The Worst Household Ornament
The Least Successful Day Trip
The Least Top-Secret Base
The Slowest Postal Delivery
How to Visit Loved Ones
The Least Comprehensible Legislation
The Least Well-Planned Robbery
The Least Successful Mugging
Our Own Chess Master
The Worst Cricket Team
How to Catch a Blackmailer

'A man who cannot make mistakes cannot do anything.'
Bernard's Bingo Magazine

The Least Successful Club

The Langworth Pig Club was set up to give owners
insurance for their pigs, tips on pig health and useful
talks on all matters relating to the advancement of pig
in general.

This fine club reached its peak in January 1988 when
all the members admitted that none of them owned a
pig. Most had not done so for fifteen years and some had
not even seen one during this period.

This heartening state of affairs was ruined by Mr
George Abbott, a local Methodist minister with an
interest in pig ear-piercing, who closed the club down
on the grounds that no one had attended the AGM at
his house in Barlin's Road for the second year running.

The Least Correct Astrologer

The jewel in Fleet Street's crown during the 1930s
and 1940s was the astrology column of R. H. Naylor
in the *Sunday Express*. In the space of a few weeks this
outstanding man predicted that Franco would never
rule Spain, that a united Ireland was imminent and
that 'war is not scheduled for 1939'. He explained that
'Hitler's horoscope shows he is not a war maker', while
admitting that Germany 'might at some point show an

interest in regaining Togoland'.

On the domestic front he predicted a general election on 7 November 1938, at which the government would gain a slender majority. The next election did not take place until 1945 and it was a landslide victory for the Labour Party.

With his unique insights into the future Naylor foresaw that 'Bolshevism and Nazism would co-operate' and said so days before Germany invaded Russia. He also predicted that 'aircraft which cannot hover will soon be deemed utterly useless' and that 'Iceland will become a key area'.

The Least Accurate Index

So often indexes are nothing more than dull signposts to a book's contents. In 1981, however, the index in the *Gardener's World Vegetable Book* transcended mere utilitarianism and was hailed as a work of art in its own right, because it bore no resemblance to the book's contents whatsoever.

Page 25, for example, is not devoted to Avoncrisp lettuce at all, but to helpful hints on planting tubers with a trowel. Furthermore, page 52 is not remotely connected with chickweed, being obsessed with the altogether more absorbing topic of cures for cabbage root fly.

The index is particularly fond of page 16 and sends readers there on no fewer than fifteen occasions, seeking aubergines, broad beans, two strains of beetroot (Avon-early and Boltardy), cloches, courgettes, cucumber, deep bed method, lettuce, uses of the Melbourne frame, marrow, melon, early peas, peppers, sweetcorn and bush tomatoes. The page is, in fact, solely concerned with the humble cabbage.

Of the 177 entries listed a magnificent 166 give bold directions to the wrong pages.

The Least Successful Tourist Resort

Tired of its reputation as Britain's least attractive town, the inhabitants of Slough decided to relaunch the place as a tourist resort. In October 1987 they bombarded the nation with advertising for 'a dream weekend in Slough' that asked, 'Why bother with Paris, Venice or Mustique when you can spend a once-in-a-lifetime weekend in Slough, the Cannes of the North and the Hollywood of Berkshire for only £75?'

'Pig out on the world's best junk food,' said the leaflets, offering a unique package break at the Holiday Inn with a weekly season ticket to the local Maybox cinema.

The price included a tour of Slough Trading Estate, Slough Community Centre ('once famous as the home base of the Ada Umsworth Old Formation Dance Team') and the car park next to the Mars bar factory, 'which was used as the location for a dramatic scene in a seven-minute sci-fi film made in 1986 by a student at the National Film School'.

Not a single enquiry was received.

The Not Terribly Good Samaritan

Being a kind-hearted sort of chap, Mr Hugh Pike rushed to the aid of a British family in distress in 1978.

They were on holiday in Bordeaux. Their Morris estate car had broken down. They needed a spare part from Britain so they had to abandon the vehicle. They spoke no French. They could not get back to Boulogne for the boat home. It was now Sunday night and the father had to be at work in his native Sheffield by 8 a.m. the next morning. The situation was almost perfect.

Wishing to help, Mr Pike told them he had a working knowledge of French, was himself going to Paris and would be only too pleased to help. He drove them at high speed to the Gare du Nord, arrived with seconds to spare, went to the ticket desk, asked a guard for the train to Boulogne, dashed down platform 6, and got the Sheffield family on board, as the train pulled out amid dewy-eyed protestations of undying gratitude and friendship.

Only as he walked back down the platform, aglow with the knowledge of a good deed done, did he look up at the departures board and realise that he had put them on the train to Bologna in Italy, a country with whose ways and languages they were even less well acquainted.

The Least Successful Men's Rights Group

Inspired by the success of the American Coalition of Free Men (it has eight hundred affiliated groups and regular meetings to campaign for men's rights), Mr Arthur Murray decided in 1983 to set up a UK branch. Since then it has attracted no members whatsoever. The regular newsletter consists of Arthur pleading with his six best friends to join.

When a reporter from *The Times* went to investigate the 'group', he found that Arthur was under constant attack from his wife, a veteran feminist who is bigger than he is, owns the house, supports Arthur financially and makes him do all the housework.

The Worst Household Ornament

For thirty years Mrs Doreen Burley polished her favourite ornament every day. She allowed her five grandchildren to play with it and usually gave the brass orb pride of place on the mantelpiece at her home in Rawtenstall, Lancashire.

Only in March 1988 did she discover it was a live bomb. When she described her pride and joy to the manager of an antique shop, he advised her to call the police.

The army arrived next day and carried it off as though it was priceless china. 'I just couldn't believe I had been polishing a bomb all this time,' Mrs Burley said. 'I must have picked it up in a box of brasses in Bradford.'

The Least Successful Day Trip

Few people have packed more into a day trip than Michael and Lillian Long of Kent who went to Boulogne in May 1987. On Easter Sunday this adventurous couple went for a short walk around the town. In no time they were spectacularly lost and showing all the qualities of born explorers.

'We walked and walked,' Mrs Long recalled, 'and the further we walked to try to get back, the further we walked away from Boulogne.'

They walked throughout the night and finally hitched a lift next morning to a small village they did not recognise. Here they caught a train to Paris. In the pleasure-loving French capital they spent all their remaining money on capturing what they thought was the train to Boulogne. After an enjoyable trip they arrived in Luxembourg at midnight on Monday.

Two hours later police put them on the train back to Paris, but it divided and their half ended up in Basel, an attractive medieval town in the north of Switzerland.

Having no money, they tried to find work but without success. The rail authorities offered them a free warrant back to Belfort, thinking this was where they had come from, whereupon this intrepid pair walked forty-two miles to Vesoul, hitched a lift to Paris and nearly boarded the train for Bonn in Germany.

Diverted to the right platform, they reached Boulogne a week after they had set out on their walk. When he arrived back at Dover, Mr Long said this was their first trip abroad and they would not be leaving England again.

The Least Top-Secret Base

RAF Caerwent was a NATO base shrouded in the utmost mystery. What was it for? What was in there? Why was it so secret?

No one knew – until a rambler's map for the district was produced showing every last detail of the base with an exact scale drawing of its layout, including the highly sensitive arms depot.

The map was produced by the Forestry Commission in 1976 from a series of aerial photographs. When the Ministry of Defence found out and banned the map five years later, two thousand copies had already been sold to enthusiastic ramblers and holidaymakers.

The Slowest Postal Delivery

So infuriated was Mr J. F. Brown of Hampstead, London, by the sex manuals that had appeared on his local library's shelves that he sat down straight away to write a letter of complaint, dated 14 July 1938.

Trembling with indignation, he immediately posted his irate missive, which suggested that 'all these disgusting books by Havelock Ellis and similarly dirty-minded men posing as psychiatrists be removed from your shelves. Nay Sir, I do more than suggest it, I demand it. You are contributing to the undermining of the fibre of the English people. And if war comes, as it most certainly will, we shall be in no state to wage it.'

Although the library was only a mile away from his home address, his letter arrived in 1976, thirty-eight years, seven months, five weeks and one day later, by which time the librarian had died and the library had been closed in a merger with Camden.

How to Visit Loved Ones

The art of visiting relatives was significantly enhanced by Dr John Fellows in March 1984. Having bought a £600 return air ticket to New York, he flew to John F. Kennedy Airport. On arrival, however, he found that he could not remember his daughter's address.

Most of us could have managed this, but Dr Fellows went one further and, pulling that little bit extra out of the bag, found that he was also unable to remember her name. Thus equipped, he spent several hours at the airport trying to recall it before catching the next plane home. 'I was tired,' he explained modestly.

The Least Comprehensible Legislation

An exciting new contender for this title is the law defining how dentists should work out their salaries:

The following paragraph shall be substituted for

paragraph (ii) of regulation three of the amended regulations:

(ii) in any succeeding month in the same year the remuneration shall not exceed such sum as will, when added to the remuneration of the previous months of the year, amount to the product of the standard sum multiplied by the number of months of the year which will have expired at the end of the month in respect of which the calculation is being made together with one half of any authorised fees in excess of that product which but for the provisions of this regulation would have been payable in those months, excluding for all the purposes of this paragraph the month of January 1949.

This is still not, however, quite equal to the classic regulation concerning groundnuts:

in the nuts (unground), (other than groundnuts) order, the expression nuts shall have reference to such nuts, other than ground nuts, as would but for this amending order not qualify as nuts (unground) (other than ground nuts) by reason of their being nuts (unground).

The Least Well-Planned Robbery

Three thieves at Billericay, Essex, gave hours of thought in 1971 to raiding the post office in Mountnessing Road.

After painstaking research they discovered the times at which there was most cash and fewest security guards on the premises. They also invested in masks, guns and a getaway car.

At a prearranged time the Mountnessing gang sped through Billericay and screeched to a halt outside the post office.

It was only when they jumped out of the car and ran towards the building that they discovered the one detail that they had omitted to check.

The post office had been closed for twelve years. 'We became a general store in 1959,' said the store's manageress, seventy-six-year-old Mrs Gertrude Haylock. She later remarked, 'I saw these two men running towards the shop with shotguns and I said to my customer, "Here is somebody having a lark."'

Making the best of an unpromising situation, the raiders pointed their guns at Mrs Haylock and her customer, Mrs Constance Clark, and demanded the contents of the till.

'I told them we had not taken any money that morning and there was only six pound in the till, so they took that. I should think it was a bit of a disappointment to them. They looked so funny dressed up like that. It was just like in a film.'

After the robbers left, the customer fainted on realising that she had been present at an incident.

The Least Successful Mugging

In 1978 Sussex police launched a hunt for a 'six-foot, dark-haired youth of about twenty' who failed to mug a five-foot, seventy-four-year-old grandmother.

The youth sprang upon Mrs Ethel West while she was walking through Chichester Cathedral cloisters. The result should have been a foregone conclusion. Surprisingly, however, when Mrs West grabbed the mugger's wrist, he cried, 'Oh God! Oh no! Stop!'

Encouraged by these pleas, she put him in an arm lock at which the mugger cried, 'Oh no. Oh Christ!' and ran away.

'If I hadn't been carrying my shopping, I would really have put him on his back,' said Mrs West, who took a course in judo when younger.

'Before my husband died I used to practise throwing him at Christmas,' she explained.

Our Own Chess Master

To his utter amazement Mr Geoffrey Hosking, an Englishman studying at Moscow University, was invited to take part in part in the highly prestigious 1965 Baku International Tournament for chess masters. He did not regard himself as a chess player and had only rarely played the game.

It transpired that they were short of foreign players and a Russian friend had put his name forward on the strength of Hosking's vodka-fuelled victory in a casual friendly game that neither of them could remember with any clarity.

Hosking not only lost all twelve games in Baku, but also played them in such a way that the Tournament

Bulletin refused to publish the customary match details on the grounds that they were incredible.

The Worst Cricket Team

Formed in 1950 at University College, Oxford, the Utopers XI played for thirty-three years before conceding their first victory. Explaining their team's astonishing consistency, the college handbooks said: 'It is not the winning, but the taking part that counts. Indeed, what alternative was there?'

The 1980 season got off at the usual cracking pace with well-deserved defeats by Mansfield College, the London Utopers, New College and the Captain Scott Invitation XI. They kept this standard up throughout their annual tour of Dorchester-on-Thames.

Then the unbelievable happened. According to the college magazine, 'The Utopers' spirits came in for a severe blow when they met the combined forces of the Southern Counties Open University XI, a team genuinely more dedicated to playing the game for the game's sake. For once victory could not be staved off despite gallant attempts from all concerned.'

Their nerve was broken and from that day the Utopers went on to a series of wins. So appalled were the older players that in 1988 the original team was planning to re-form in order to recapture their lost verve.

How to Catch a Blackmailer

In February 1988 an anonymous caller rang the police to say that he would leave poisoned chocolate bars all over Lincolnshire if they did not deposit £50,000 in the phone box at the village of Harpswell.

Sensing an easy arrest, the police left this sum in a briefcase and retired to lie in wait. At the appointed time they sprang from the bushes and pounced on an innocent villager who had come from the local caravan park to telephone his mother. In their enthusiasm to frogmarch him off to justice, they forgot their briefcase and so returned to find that the real blackmailer had now taken it.

Seeing a distant figure, the police dashed off and arrested a second blameless villager as he walked across a field to the nearby local social club.

After six hours of cross-examination the Regional Crime Squad said he had been the 'unfortunate victim of circumstance'.

14

ENCOURAGING NEWS FROM THE UNITED STATES OF AMERICA

The Least Successful Statue
The Worst American Poet
The Least Successful Awards Ceremony
Baton Twirling Latest
The Least Successful Memorial
The Least Successful Acrobat
The Worst Celebrations
The Least Successful Flight to Los Angeles
The Least Successful Buffalo Chip Throwing Contest
The Worst Quiz Show
The Least Successful Community Centre
The Burglar Who Could Not Get Out
The Least Successful Top Secret
The Least Successful Opening Ceremony
New Advances in American Football
The Least Satisfactory Election
The Least Successful Fire-Proofing
The Worst Baseball Team
The Least Successful Suicide Attempt

'The history of mankind is an immense sea of errors in which a few obscure truths may here and there be found.'

MARQUIS DE BECCARIA

The Least Successful Statue

In 1972 Mr W. M. Riesk of Salt Lake City commissioned a working model of Abraham Lincoln. It had two thousand computerised parts and three hundred movements, including breathing, heartbeats and a life-like mouth through which came a speech pre-recorded by the Hollywood actor Royal Dano.

At the start of a four-year, coast-to-coast tour of shopping precincts, the statue was erected at the Northgate Centre in Seattle. A large crowd gathered round, expecting to hear Lincoln's celebrated address, which includes the line, 'What is it that we hold most dear amongst us? Our own liberty and prosperity.'

However, all thirty-one channels of the computer were jammed by signals from the local rock-and-roll radio station and what actually came out of the President's lips were the words:

> I wanna tell ya I can hardly speak.
> I wanna get off, mamma.
> I can hardly feel the pain no more.
> I wanna get my rocks.

Having identified this as the Rolling Stones, Mr Riesk called in an electrician from Los Angeles, who improved things no end. After twenty-one hours of work Lincoln had lost his voice altogether and was only able to breathe out.

The statue continued its national tour silent and sitting still. Mr Riesk said that he was carrying on because 'I am patriotic. I even cry when I hear "The Star-Spangled Banner".'

The Worst American Poet

Julia Moore, 'the Sweet Singer of Michigan' (1847–1920) was so bad that Mark Twain said her first book gave him joy for twenty years.

Her verse is mainly concerned with violent death – the Great Fire of Chicago and the yellow fever epidemic proved natural subjects for her pen.

Whether the death was by drowning, by fits or by a runaway sleigh, the formula was the same:

> Have you heard of the dreadful fate
> Of Mr P. P. Bliss and wife?
> Of their death I will relate,
> And also others lost their life
> (in the) Ashbula Bridge disaster,
> Where so many people died.

Even if you started out reasonably healthy in one of Julia's poems, the chances are that after a few stanzas you would be at the bottom of a river or struck by lightning. A critic of the day said she was 'worse than a Gatling gun' and in one slim volume counted twenty-one killed and nine wounded.

Incredibly some papers were critical of the work, even

suggesting that the Sweet Singer was 'semi-literate'. Her reply was forthright: 'The editors that has spoken in this scandalous manner, have went beyond reason.' She added that 'literary work is very difficult to do'.

The Least Successful Awards Ceremony

The American Institute of Architects held their 1979 annual conference in Kansas City so as to be near the Kemper Arena, to which they had awarded their prize as 'one of the finest buildings in the nation'.

On the first day of the conference hordes of architects toured this inspired structure with its wide spanning roof trusses, which the *Architectural Record* described as having 'an almost awesome muscularity'.

On the second day it fell down, filling the entire zone with a dramatic heap of tangled metal work.

Baton Twirling Latest

Noted for the height, range and drama of their twirls, members of the Ventura Baton Twirling Troupe surprised even themselves on one occasion in the late 1960s.

During an Independence Day march past, one of their batons hit a power cable, blacked out the area, started a grass fire and put the local radio station off the air. 'They were on form,' the mayor said.

The Least Successful Memorial

The building of a new staff canteen in 1977 gave the US Department of Agriculture the opportunity to commemorate a famous nineteenth-century Colorado pioneer.

Amid a blaze of enthusiastic publicity the Agriculture Secretary, Robert Bergland, opened 'The Alfred Packer Memorial Dining Facility', with the words: 'Alfred Packer exemplifies the spirit and fare that this Agriculture Department canteen will provide.'

Several months later the cafeteria was renamed when it was discovered that Packer was a cannibal, who had been convicted of murdering and eating five prospectors in 1874.

The Least Successful Acrobat

When the circus came to New York in 1978, the publicity posters carried the question: 'Can aerialist Tito Gaona – spinning at seventy miles an hour – accomplish the most difficult acrobatic feat of the twentieth century?' The short answer to this was: 'No.'

Every night for nine months Tito attempted the first ever quadruple somersault in mid-air from a flying trapeze sixty feet above the ground. Every night for nine months he got part way through, missed his catcher and plunged into the safety net. At Madison Square Gardens he sustained a full season of magnificent failure.

Asked if he had ever done it, Tito replied, 'Yes, once. At rehearsals and only my family were watching.'

The Worst Celebrations

Human Kindness Day took place in Washington DC on 10 May 1975. At a press conference afterwards police said there had been 600 arrests, 150 smashed windows, 42 looted refreshment stands, 17 stonings of uniformed officers, 33 fires and 120 cases of public brawling. Furthermore, 14 cars had been demolished in Constitution Avenue.

Miss Carol Kirkendall, a spokeswoman for the organisers, said that 'although the sporadic rock-throwing, public mayhem and purse-snatchings had been a sadness, a lot of beautiful things were going on out there'.

The Least Successful Flight to Los Angeles

In 1938 Douglas 'Wrong Way' Corrigan was given a tickertape welcome down Broadway after flying across the Atlantic by mistake. On 16 July he boarded his nine-year-old monoplane, which cost him £150, intending to fly to Los Angeles. Onlookers at the Floyd Bennet Airfield in New York noticed, however, that, instead of turning westward as expected, he took an easterly direction shortly after take-off in thick fog.

Twenty-eight hours, thirteen minutes later, he landed at Baldonnel Aerodrome near Dublin, where the airport manager said it was 'a great day for the Irish'. On arrival, Mr Corrigan said that he was 'pretty tired', having travelled at 90 mph equipped only with a pressure gauge, a compass and a map of the United States of America. He did not take any food supplies. 'I want to do this trip again,' he told astonished reporters.

In America he was hailed as 'another Lindbergh' and New York Irish groups argued for several days over the right to organise the welcoming reception. Manhattan won and gathered twenty other Corrigans, mostly policemen, to greet their namesake. Parades and speeches lasted all day.

The Least Successful Buffalo Chip Throwing Contest

The National Buffalo Chip Throwing Contest* of 1979 at Athol in Maryland got off to a cracking start when organisers failed to appreciate that there were no buffaloes for five hundred miles, that no excrement chips were available except on emergency order by air freight and that the airline at Laramie, Wyoming, had refused to carry them on grounds of hygiene.

Cowpats were officially ruled a suitable substitute. At this point a contestant, Dr Philip Ball of Muncie, Indiana, arrived with bursitis in his throwing shoulder.

* Footnote for non-American students: It is the practice of cowpokes with free time in the USA to hurl 100 per cent organic buffalo faeces in a competitive spirit. Distances of anything up to 250 feet can be attained.

During Dr Ball's first lob he developed 'sudden malfunction of gyro control', whereupon the chip turned through a 90-degree angle and knocked out the event judge. His second lob shattered in mid-air showering much of the audience, who began to go home.

Dr Ball sustained this level of performance throughout. He not only came 23rd out of 23, but also won the award for Mr Congeniality and for the cow chip thrower with the best mental attitude.

The Worst Quiz Show

The worst quiz show ever broadcast on television was *You're in the Picture*, which graced American screens in January 1961. It was taken off by universal acclaim after one instalment.

The programme was hosted by Jackie Gleason, who habitually signs his letters 'The Great Gleason'. It is now possible to see why. In this show, celebrity panellists had to stick their head through holes in a plyboard screen and ask him questions in order to discover what was painted on the other side.

Due to the fascinating obscurity of these scenes ('The Raising of the Old Glory at Sqirri Barri', for example) there was no way that a guest could identify them unless equipped with the most advanced psychic abilities.

On the next week's show Mr Gleason pitched up on his own.

'Ladies and gentlemen,' he said, 'I think you'll notice that there is no panel tonight.' Furthermore, there was a 100 per cent absence of painted plyboard scenes. Instead he sat there, drinking a cup of coffee that was 'chock-full-o-booze' while saying what a flop last week's show had been.

After a thirty-minute post-mortem, interlaced with jokes and personal reminiscences, he said, 'I don't know what we're going to do, but tune in next week for the greatest soapless opera you've ever seen.'

Audiences could hardly wait for next week's show when the host once again appeared on his own until joined by a chimpanzee. It was not until the third instalment that he risked having another human on the show, by which time Kellogg's had withdrawn sponsorship on the grounds that it was no longer a quiz programme.

The Least Successful Community Centre

The runaway champion in this category is the $280,000 Merrill Township Community Centre in Michigan, which opened in 1976 and had no visitors whatsoever. It was eventually discovered three years later, having collapsed under a load of snow, by a solitary woodsman who was out shooting rabbits.

A spokesman for the project said that although it planned a full programme of counselling, barn dances and literacy classes designed to create a new community spirit in remotest Michigan, it was 'built in the middle of a virtually inaccessible forest' and money ran out for the road.

The Burglar Who Could Not Get Out

A trail-blazing burglar broke into a vast mansion on millionaire's row in June 1982 at Bel Air, Los Angeles. While on a sack-filling tour of this palatial structure, he went through the ballroom into the hall, down the escalators to the single-lane swimming arbour, up to the library across the dining room, out of the annexe and into the conservatory containing sixty-three varieties of tropical plant and a cage full of sulphur-crested parrots.

Deciding that now was the time to make a quick exit, he went back through the dining room, up to the gymnasium across the indoor tennis court, down a spiral staircase to an enclosed patio with synchronised fountains, out to the cocktail lounge through junior's soundproofed drum studio and back into the room full of increasingly excited parrots who normally saw nobody from one day to the next.

Panicking slightly, he ran back towards the library, through swing doors into a gallery containing the early works of Jackson Pollock, out through the kitchen across a jacuzzi enclosure and up two flights of stairs, at which point he became hysterical, ran outside along the balcony around the circular corridors, up more stairs, down the landing into the master bedroom and woke up the owners to ask them how to get out.

In order to spare him further distress, they arranged for a local policeman to escort him from the premises.

The Least Successful Top Secret

The F-19 Stealth fighter plane was so secret that not even American senators voting for its billion-dollar development were allowed to see the plans.

It was so secret that when an F-19 crashed in the Sequoia National Park, California, the Defence Department put a news blackout on the event, stationed armed guards around the area and sent aircraft to patrol for intruders.

It was so secret that the Pentagon refused even to acknowledge the existence of the so-called 'invisible fighter'.

In July 1986 Testor Toys innocently produced a model kit for the F-19 and a hundred thousand children bought them in high street stores for around ten dollars each. When the facts were pointed out to the manufacturers, they said, 'You've got to have a bit of mystery about it. That makes it exciting.'

The Least Successful Opening Ceremony

Wishing to open their new pistol range in style, officials of Brigham City decided in 1975 to invite a team of crack marksman from the Utah Peace Force. The idea was that one of them would step forward and break the ceremonial ribbon with a single bullet.

It was a complete triumph. Five hundred bullets later the ribbon remained impressively unspoiled. According to an eyewitness, it was cut only when an officer stepped forward and 'let go with a shotgun' at point-blank range, leaving the ribbon in smouldering shreds.

New Advances in American Football

The greatest ever exponent of American football was Jim Marshall of the Minnesota Vikings. On 26 October 1964 in a match against the San Francisco 49-ers he crowned a glorious career by snatching a 49-er fumble, sprinting sixty yards the wrong way down the Kezar Stadium and scoring for the opposition. This sort of touchdown is much harder to achieve because you have to beat the defensive attempts of not only the opposing side, but also your own team.

No one could believe this marvellous display of skill and in no time the entire Minnesota bench was chasing down the sideline, waving their arms at him wildly. With his mind very much on the job, Marshall said that he 'didn't hear anybody yelling', but construed his colleagues' behaviour as understandable excitement.

With a modesty that is common to all great athletes he said, 'I just picked the ball up and started running. I guess I just got turned around.'

The Least Satisfactory Election

In 1986 the electors of San Matteo County, California, voted for Mr Brendan Maguire to be sheriff with an overwhelming 81,679 majority.

Only when the results were announced did anyone point out that Mr Maguire had been dead for two months.

His continuing popularity was due to his legendary performance in the 1948 Gaelic Cup Final when his side was heavily defeated by a team that included his brother.

The Least Successful Fire-Proofing

The world's first fire-proof theatre, the Iroquois, opened in Chicago on 1 December 1903.

Just thirty days later, as a double octet was launching into a close harmony version of 'In the Pale Moonlight', a faulty blue light bulb used to create a subtle lunar effect set fire to the scenery. The safety curtain jammed two-thirds of the way down; the audience was asked to leave, and the theatre burned to the ground.

The Worst Baseball Team

Formed in 1962, the New York Mets were given a tickertape welcome down Broadway before they had even touched the ball.

On 13 April the Department of Sanitation band struck up 'Hey, Look Me Over' and forty thousand spectators lined the route as the uniformed players rode past like conquering heroes in a rainbow-coloured procession of fourteen convertibles. Along the route ten thousand mock baseballs and bats were thrown into the crowd.

After this triumphant start they really got cracking and by 22 April they had equalled the Brooklyn Dodgers' 1918 record of losing nine games in a row. And by the end of this great debut they had lost more matches in one season than anyone else in the history of the game. The final figure was an impressive 120 defeats.

The Least Successful Suicide Attempt

Tired of life and its assorted awfulness, Mrs Elvita Adams decided in 1979 to jump off the 86th floor of the Empire State Building. She said 'goodbye' to the world and leapt, whereupon a sudden gust of wind blew her back into the 85th floor, merely invigorated by the fresh air and exercise.

15

1980: A VINTAGE YEAR

The Least Successful Fun Festival
The Worst Production of *Macbeth*
The Least Successful Oil Drillers
The Worst Rugby League Team
The Least Successful Demolition
The Least Successful Agony Aunt
The Least Satisfactory Robot
The Least Successful Wedding Reception
The Plan That Failed
The Least Successful Wedding Toast
The Least Successful Attempt to Murder a Spouse

'It's awful. You'll like it.'
Cabaret

The Least Successful Fun Festival

In October 1980 Chichester hosted a fun festival that promised 'a weekend that was different'. The organisers kept their word.

The British all-comers dogs swimming race was called off when not a single owner entered his pet; the pie-eating contest was won by a man who consumed just three and a half pies; the helicopter rides were cancelled because of bad weather; the parachute display was called off because the landing site was too close to the A27; the Elvis Presley lookalike, 'Rupert', was delayed by a road accident and when he eventually arrived there were so few spectators the act was shelved.

When by three o'clock nothing had happened at all, a lively crowd formed around the organisers' tent. Inexplicably, they were not enjoying this feast of entertainment. Loud among the voices of complaint was that of Mr R. Farncombe, who had come all the way from West Worthing: 'I went mostly to see Rupert who was not there, for a helicopter ride we never got and wrestling which did not exist. Thank goodness we didn't arrive till 12.30.' He was offered free tickets for the next day when the high spot was a hot-air balloon that failed to turn up.

The Worst Production of *Macbeth*

In September 1980 crowds poured into the Old Vic Theatre in London to see Peter O'Toole's unforgettable *Macbeth*, which is widely held to have basked in the worst set of theatrical notices in modern times.

Eradicating the unnecessarily tragic aspects that have always weighed the play down, the cast sent the first-night audience home rocking with happy laughter. One critic after another rose up to acknowledge the astonishing qualities of this production.

The greatest acclaim was reserved for the unexpected qualities of Mr O'Toole's performance.

The *Daily Mail* observed that 'it was, of course, the rottenest luck for him to run smack into a wall on his third bravura exit (so much of the play takes place in the dark)'.

Another critic noticed that the three glamorous witches were not 'foul, unnatural hags', as Shakespeare absurdly suggests. Dressed in white chiffon gowns, they 'look as if they shop at Fortnum and Mason's'.

The London *Evening News* critic drew attention to the new-age Lady Macbeth who 'greeted her husband by leaping at him and achieving a leg-encircling embrace of the kind which illustrates helpful sex manuals'. The general dramatic style, he said, 'would have woken the whole castle'.

In no time coach parties began arriving at the Old Vic where the run was soon sold out. From the London and provincial runs it earned a quarter of a million pounds, making it one of the most profitable *Macbeth*s on record. 'I was born to play this part,' Mr O'Toole said later.

The Least Successful Oil Drillers

Erecting the very latest equipment, Texaco workmen set about drilling for oil at Lake Peigneur in Louisiana during November 1980.

After only three hours' drilling they sat back expecting oil to shoot up. Instead, however, they watched a whirlpool form, sucking down not only the entire 1,300-acre lake, but also five houses, nineteen barges, eight tugboats, two oil rigs, a mobile home, most of a botanical garden and 10 per cent of nearby Jefferson Island, leaving a half-mile-wide crater. No one told them there was an abandoned salt mine underneath.

A local fisherman said he thought the world was coming to an end.

The Worst Rugby League Team

The outstanding contribution of Doncaster to sporting life can never be overlooked. In 1975 it produced a rugby league team that was acknowledged as the worst professional sports side in the world. There can be no higher praise.

They have been bottom of the league more times than any other club and in 1977 they set a new all-comers' record for the longest losing run of 40 consecutive games. A television documentary was made recording the team's unquenchable spirit. It revealed that they do not recognise their own jerseys in muddy conditions and often tackle each other.

Their philosophical manager, Mr Tom Norton, said, 'When they lose I don't mind, so long as they entertain us. And, you know, it is possible to excite people even if you are getting thrashed.'

After a streaker had run topless across the field at Twickenham before an international match, Doncaster advertised in the local paper for a woman with a 42-inch bust do likewise at their own ground, Tatty's Field, in a last-ditch attempt to attract a crowd. 'We would quite happily settle for anything from 38 inches upwards,' Mr Norton said when there was no immediate response.

In 1980 they became the first ever club to put their whole team up for sale. Two days later their manager said, 'We haven't had any enquiries yet.'

The Least Successful Demolition

In December 1980 Solihull Council hired a local firm of contractors to demolish a row of dilapidated cowsheds on Stratford Road near Birmingham.

Early on Sunday morning eyewitnesses saw an excavator moving at speed along the road. When it came to the cowsheds, it turned off the wrong side and headed without pause for Monkspath Hall, a listed eighteenth-century building set in fields with a tree-lined approach and rated as one of the most famous farmhouses in the Midlands.

In forty-five minutes the building was reduced to a heap of rubble.

The Least Successful Agony Aunt

This honour falls to the outstanding Rose Shepherd who wrote the agony column on *Honey* magazine in 1980. From the day of her appointment onwards she did not receive a single reader's letter. When, months later, a few actually did arrive, this fine woman announced that she could not solve any of them.

'They asked impossible questions like "I eat cigarette tobacco. Is this wrong?" It was hopeless.' Deciding that people's problems are basically insoluble, she resigned.

The Least Satisfactory Robot

Seeking greater efficiency, the Kavio restaurant in Leith bought Donic, a robot programmed as a wine waiter. In the summer of 1980 they dressed it in a black hat and bow tie, fitted the batteries and turned it on.

Showing a natural flair for the work, this advanced machine ran amok, smashed the furniture, poured wine all over the carpet and frightened the diners until its lights went out, its voice box packed up and its head dropped off in a customer's lap.

When asked to account for this outstanding performance, the robot's manufacturer said that he had given the operating instructions to the restaurant's disc-jockey.

The Least Successful Wedding Reception

Newly-weds John and Barbara Besio claimed this record at the Blue Dolphin restaurant in Los Angeles during 1980.

The reception made a promising start when the groom's father expressed the wish to dance on the table. So unbridled was this performance that the manager called the police. In the resulting fracas five policemen were injured and six wedding guests arrested.

At this point the bride asked what kind of family she was marrying into, whereupon the groom departed from the usual custom, picked up the entire wedding cake and pushed it in her face. When fighting broke out between the happy couple, the police were called again and threatened to arrest them.

Guests waving off the newly-weds in the going-away car noticed that Mrs Besio, as we must now call her, landed a blow that appeared temporarily to stun her husband, bringing peace to an otherwise perfect occasion.

The Plan That Failed

The plan: one night in May 1980 David Barber would enter Cheltenham Co-op with a bag full of equipment to break into a steel and reinforced-concrete safe. After removing countless thousands he would hide them, with his equipment, in his bag and make his escape disguised in a jogging suit bought specially for the occasion.

What actually happened: he broke into the Co-op and was drilling away from the moment he arrived until shortly before dawn. He was just going through the last metal barrier when the door swung open of its own accord, having been unlocked throughout. The safe turned out to be empty. When he made his getaway next morning his bag was found in its hiding place by schoolboys who took it to the police. It was bugged ready for his return.

The Least Successful Wedding Toast

Like all proud fathers, Grigory Romanov, the Mayor of Leningrad, wanted the very best for his daughter's wedding. In January 1980 this senior member of the Soviet Politburo persuaded the Director of the city's Hermitage Museum to lend him Catherine the Great's china tea set especially for the occasion.

Late in the exuberant proceedings one guest got to his feet and accidentally dropped a cup. Thinking that this was a toast, the other guests took it as a signal for the traditional gesture of good luck, whereupon they all rose to their feet and hurled the entire service into the fireplace.

The Least Successful Attempt to Murder a Spouse

Dwarfing all known records for matrimonial homicide, Mr Peter Scott of Southsea made seven attempts to kill his wife without her once noticing that anything was wrong.

In 1980 he took out an insurance policy on his good lady that would bring him £250,000 in the event of her accidental death. Soon afterwards he placed a lethal dose of mercury in her strawberry flan, but it all rolled out. Not wishing to waste this deadly substance, he next stuffed her mackerel with the entire contents of the bottle. This time she ate it, but with no side-effects whatsoever.

Warming to the task, he then took his better half on holiday to Yugoslavia. Recommending the panoramic views, he invited her to sit on the edge of a cliff. She declined to do so, prompted by what she later described as some 'sixth sense'. The same occurred only weeks later when he urged her to savour the view from Beachy Head.

While his spouse was in bed with chickenpox he started a fire outside her bedroom door, but some interfering busybody put it out. Undeterred, he started another fire and burned down the entire flat at Taswell Road, Southsea. The wife of his bosom escaped uninjured.

Another time he asked her to stand in the middle of the road so that he could drive towards her and check if his brakes were working.

At no time did Mrs Scott feel that the magic had gone out of their marriage. Since it appeared that nothing short of a small nuclear bomb would have alerted this good woman to her husband's intentions, he eventually gave up and confessed everything to the police.

16

THE SPIRIT OF THE OLYMPICS

Marathons Can Be Fun
The Worst Pentathlon Team
The Slowest Olympic Athlete
The Slowest Start to an Olympic Heat
The Worst Ski Jumper
The Least Successful Olympic Swimmer
The Least Successful Attempt to Break an
Olympic Record
The Least Successful Hero's Return

'Every decision you make is a mistake.'
EDWARD DAHLBERG

'Success: the one unpardonable sin against
one's fellow man.'
AMBROSE BIERCE

Marathons Can Be Fun

In 1966 Shizo Kanakuri set a new record for the Olympic marathon. At Stockholm he completed the 26.2-mile course in an unbeatable fifty-four years, eight months, six days, eight hours, thirty-two minutes and 20.3 seconds, having started in 1912.

He had run several miles before passing a group of people having a very pleasant drink in their front garden. As he was suffering from chronic heat exhaustion at the time he did the only sensible thing and tottered over to join them. Being a sociable sort of man, he stayed for a few more drinks whereupon he changed his race tactics dramatically, caught a train back to Stockholm, booked into a hotel for the night, boarded the next boat to Japan, got married, had six children and ten grandchildren, before returning to the villa where he had stopped and completing the marathon for the honour of Japan.

The Worst Pentathlon Team

Only Tunisia has really explored the possibilities of modern pentathlon, in which athletes show quite unnecessary prowess in five different sports.

At the 1960 Rome Olympics they scored no points

at all in the equestrian event because the entire team fell off their horses. It was the first time that anyone had scored 0 at the Olympics.

Encouraged by this start, they hit sizzling form in the swimming, where one of their people nearly drowned and the versatile Ennachi (who had already fallen off a horse) took twice as long to complete a mere 300 metres as the winner. Their shooting was described as 'wild' and they were ordered from the rifle range because they were endangering the lives of the judges.

When it came to the fencing, only one of their team could do it, so they kept sending the same man out. During the third bout his opponent said, 'I've fought you before', ripped off his visor and had him disqualified.

Tunisia came a splendid 17th out of 17. They were a spectacular nine thousand points behind the leaders and scored half as many as Germany who came sixteenth. It is the lowest ever pentathlon score and an example to us all.

The Slowest Olympic Athlete

At the 1976 Olympics in Montreal, Olmeus Charles from Haiti was last by the largest margin ever recorded. He set an all-time record for the 10,000-metres race. Giving the crowd tremendous value for money, he completed the course in 42 minutes 11 seconds. Everyone lapped him at least three times and the winner finished so far ahead he would have had time to complete another 5,000 metres.

An argument broke out among the track officials as to whether he should be allowed to finish the course. Happily, the crowd was not denied this fine sight and the entire Olympic timetable was held up by 14 minutes.

The Slowest Start to an Olympic Heat

A relaxing start is, of course, essential to anyone who really wants to enjoy a race. The finest such start was achieved by the American athletes Eddie Hart and Ray Robinson, who held the 100-metres world record and would not normally interest us. In 1972, however, they pulled out something a little bit extra, missed the bus from the Olympic village and watched their own race on television. This gave them a much fuller overall sense of the whole event.

The Worst Ski Jumper

Few people know who won the 90-metres ski jump at the 1988 Winter Olympics in Calgary. Everyone, however, knows that Eddie 'the Eagle' Edwards came a definitive last, flapping both arms for mid-air balance and complaining that he could not see anything because his pebble spectacles steamed up during take-off.

A plasterer from Cheltenham, he amazed everyone by deciding to enter the Olympics after several practice runs on the local dry ski slope.

His fame went before him and a huge, cheering crowd

met him at the airport when his plane arrived late and his bag split open so that every piece of his gear went round and round the luggage carousel with Eddie in hot pursuit.

Next morning he found that his ski bindings had been crushed and so he missed his first two practice jumps while they were repaired. He got in one jump and survived only to find that he was locked out of his cabin with all his clothes inside.

When he did get to the media centre, he was not allowed into his own press conference because he did not have the right credentials.

Known as 'the barmy Brit', he soon gained a huge following throughout the world. Millions watched his jump and when he landed he raised his arms in a victory salute normally reserved for the outright winner.

A living embodiment of the Olympic spirit, he said that he did not train in the gym because it made him ache. He was later invited on to a chat show with Burt Reynolds and driven around his home town in an open-top bus so that ecstatic multitudes could get a glimpse of him.

The Least Successful Olympic Swimmer

Carolyn Schuler of the USA won the 100 metres butter-fly at the 1960 Rome Olympics in a new world-record time. She was, however, completely overshadowed by her teammate, Miss Carolyn Wood, who dived into the pool, swam one length, turned, disappeared beneath the water and gave every appearance of having become the first swimmer to drown during the Olympic Games.

Miss Wood eventually rose spluttering to the surface and grasped the lane rope, whereupon her coach dived in fully clothed to administer resuscitation. Afterwards she told eager reporters, 'I got a big mouthful of water and could not go on.'

The Least Successful Attempt to Break an Olympic Record

At the glorious 1932 Olympic Games, the Finnish athlete Iso-Hollo was hot favourite to break the world record for the 3,000 metres steeplechase. Roaring into the lead from the first lap, he was distressingly on target for a new time and turned the corner expecting to hear the bell for the final lap.

He was saved from himself by the intervention of one of the Olympic all-time greats. The official lap-counter was, thankfully, looking the wrong way, being absorbed in the decathlon pole vault near by. To his great credit, he failed to ring the bell for the last lap and the entire field kept on running, which was much better for them.

When he finally looked back, Iso-Hollo had completed the race in a much more satisfactory 10 minutes 33.4 seconds. It was the slowest ever time for the 3,000 metres steeplechase, which is really something, but they did run an extra 450 metres to make this possible.

The Least Successful Hero's Return

At the 1932 Olympics in Los Angeles, the Argentinian pugilist Santiago Alberto Lovell let everybody down by winning a gold medal for heavyweight boxing. Lovell redeemed the situation, however, on the boat trip home.

So bad was the food on board that the team appointed him to be their spokesman with the ship's captain. When the protest got nowhere, he led what was later described as a 'mutiny' in which fighting broke out. Unbiased onlookers said the Argentinian team did some of their best boxing for years in these moments, but the captain called an armed guard who kept the Olympic squad under lock and key for the rest of the voyage.

Instead of the predictable hero's welcome at Buenos Aires docks, Lovell was named as the ringleader, surrounded by armed police and carted off to jail in handcuffs.

☞ 17 ☜

STORIES I FAILED TO PIN DOWN

The Least Successful Kamikaze Pilot
The Least Successful Witch
The Burglar Who Called the Police
The Least Successful Zoo
The Least Successful Purchase of a Pet
The Worst Hammer-Throwing
The Least Ideal Couple
The Least Successful Divers
The Least Successful Motorcyclist
The Least Effective Birth Control Campaign
The Worst Labour Relations Conference
The Least Successful Slimmers
The Worst Tulip Festival
The Least Successful Audience Participation
The Least Successful Choral Contest

'The worst is not
So long as we can say, "This is the worst".'
WILLIAM SHAKESPEARE, *King Lear*, IV:1

The Least Successful Kamikaze Pilot

During the last world war a Japanese kamikaze pilot made no fewer than eleven suicide flights. Although he set off with only enough petrol for a one-way trip and no weapons of self-defence and the ritual farewell from his commanding officer, he came back safely each time and went on to write an autobiography in which he claimed that the planes were unsafe.

A member of the Japanese Special Attack Corps, he lived till he was ninety-three.

The Least Successful Witch

In 1978 a witch put a curse on Nottingham Forest Football Club. In that year they won the League Championship and the Football League Cup with the longest unbeaten run in the history of English football before going on to win the European Cup two years in succession.

The Burglar Who Called the Police

A New York burglar committed what many admirers regard as the perfect crime in 1969. Following a carefully prepared plan, he climbed up onto the roof of a supermarket which he intended to burgle.

Once there, he discovered that he could not enter the building since the skylight was marginally too small to get through.

With a sudden flash of inspiration he removed all his clothes and dropped them through the skylight intending to follow them himself seconds later. Brilliantly, he was still unable to fit through and had to call the police to get his clothes back.

The Least Successful Zoo

In 1972 a husband and wife bought a small zoo in a peaceful village near Bordeaux in south-west France. When they took over it was an ordinary zoo with nothing of interest to our sort of student. It had three hundred animals, including sixty-four bison, the largest collection of hyenas in captivity and enough Brent geese to delight the most avid fan. There next followed a prolonged period of inmate escape.

Two years later they had seventy-five animals. Bison were thin on the ground; there was only one hyena (and that was being treated for a prolapsed uterus) and there was not a Brent goose in sight. The exodus started when six old giraffes moved off, like pensioners going to the country to end their days in peace.

Unlike pensioners, however, they were chased by gendarmes all the way to the coast. After they beat it, the seals did a bunk and one called 'Flipper' was found crossing the Bordeaux–Arcachon highway.

Then all hell broke loose and for some months the town's inhabitants became accustomed to wallabies, hyenas, chimpanzees, giant pumas and all varieties of exotic birds roaming the streets.

No zookeeper has done more to spread interest in wildlife among the community and, before long, stampedes became a hazard for cyclists.

The Least Successful Purchase of a Pet

In 1980 an Italian businessman in Brescia was sent out to buy a pet dog for his children. When he returned with a small fluffy bundle, a family argument immediately broke out as to what breed it was. His wife insisted it was a fine-haired chihuahua and his children would not rest from claiming it was a poodle, while the buyer himself would hear no word against his own belief that it was a pedigree labrador, as the salesman had told him.

Only when he took the animal to the vet after three months, complaining that it never barked, did they learn that it was, in fact, a lion.

The Worst Hammer-Throwing

At an athletics event in the north-east of England during 1952 a hammer-thrower broke all known records. With a superhuman effort he swirled and let go of the hammer, which flew out of the enclosure and smashed onto the bonnet of his own Triumph Spitfire, which he had arranged to sell that night, causing £150 worth of damage, before bouncing off through the window of the athletics office and knocking out the regional organiser for hammer-throwing, who had been called away to telephone his wife.

At previous events the same athlete had hit an Esso petrol station, a police car and the gents, from which a cowering spectator had emerged with the belief that he had been struck by lightning.

The Least Ideal Couple

In 1983 a television company held a nationwide competition to find 'Britain's ideal couple'. The winning pair duly appeared in all the papers, smiling happily and giving extensive interviews about the secret of their successful relationship.

Had it ended there this unseemly bliss would merely have depressed the entire nation. The couple, however, turned out to be far more interesting than anyone would have suspected. The day before the proposed broadcast the young woman announced that their engagement was off because her fiancé had (a) smacked her face at a Lindisfarne concert and (b) kept from her the fact that he was already married to a woman called Barbara, who had thought that *they* were the ideal couple. The programme was broadcast as planned.

The Least Successful Divers

In 1979 a West Country sub-aqua club gained permission to dive in Britain's most inaccessible loch. Happy in the knowledge that they were the first ever people to explore the underwater world of remotest Scotland, they drove 740 miles, climbed 3,000 feet, put on their gear and plunged in to find that it was only four feet deep.

The Least Successful Motorcyclist

Thrilled with his new purchase in 1981, a would-be motorcyclist in Smyrna, USA, invited his best friend round to see the gleaming machine.

'Want to see how it works?' the proud owner asked.

'Sure, why not?' replied the buddy.

He cranked the engine, which roared into life, and the bike shot through sliding glass doors, dragging its owner with it.

While the ambulance was called, his wife mopped up the spilled gasoline with tissue paper and threw it down the lavatory.

When our man returned 'wrapped up like a dummy', according to the local newspaper, he went into the lavatory and, reflecting on the day, lit a cigarette. When he threw the fag end down the bowl, he was thrown against the door by the resulting explosion.

Finding him on the floor again, his wife decided to

call the ambulance once more. As he was carried out, this time face down, on a stretcher, his wife said, 'Never mind, dear, nothing else can go wrong', whereupon one of the attendants tripped over the motorcycle and our hero fell to the floor, injuring his leg.

At this moment he announced that he was putting the motorbike up for sale without ever riding it.

The Least Effective Birth Control Campaign

After twelve months an Asian birth control conference announced that its recent campaign had been 'a complete fiasco'. A subsequent survey showed that 79 per cent of the men had taken the contraceptive pill intended for women and 98 per cent had continued putting the condom on their finger, as they were shown in the demonstration.

Later that year, the Chinese minister for birth control offered to resign when it was announced that the population of this country had increased by 13 million, the equivalent of the entire population of Australia, during his two years in office.

The Worst Labour Relations Conference

A conference on 'New Ways of Bringing Harmony to the Workplace' was organised in Stockholm in the late 1970s. It was postponed when the catering union went

on strike in support of six electricians who were wrong-
fully dismissed for working to rule during a pay claim
after being asked to do more work without consultation.

The Least Successful Slimmers

Despite avid enthusiasm and regular attendance no
member of a group described as the Sheddit Slim-
ming Circle of Arkansas lost a single pound during its
sixteen-year existence. Indeed their President was com-
paratively slender when he took office, but in no time
had ballooned to the same roly-poly proportions as his
membership.

The Circle was disbanded in 1954 when they were
banned by the community centre committee. At an acri-
monious meeting the janitor said he was 'tired of clean-
ing up the mess of cake and cookie crumbs after their
sessions'.

The Worst Tulip Festival

For decades a town in the Midlands held a tulip festival
on May Day, which was the high spot of its horticul-
tural year. In 1975 the Labour Party lost control of the
Council in local elections. The in-coming Conservatives
felt that the date was far too ideological and moved it
two weeks later.

The tulips, however, were not informed and so they
flowered as usual and were all over by 14 May. The fes-

tival went ahead without them, as it was too late to withdraw the advertising.

The Least Successful Audience Participation

The growing trend towards audience involvement has given us all the opportunity to add to theatrical confusion.

During 1974 a young woman attended a performance of the rock musical *Godspell* in London.

During the interval the cast invited members of the audience up on to the stage to meet them. Sitting at the back of the theatre, she decided to leave her seat, walk down the arcade outside and pass through the stage door. After climbing a flight of dark stairs, she turned right and found herself on the brilliantly lit stage.

To the great surprise of herself and everyone else, she found herself in the middle of the cast acting *Pygmalion* at the theatre next door.

The Least Successful Choral Contest

A unique choral contest was held in Wales in the 1970s. Only one choir entered the contest and even then it only managed to come second. The choir failed to win first prize, the judges said, as a punishment for arriving forty-five minutes late.

☞ 18 ☜

THE ART OF BEING WRONG

Being wrong is a human art as old as temple decoration and ballroom dancing. No facet of life has been untouched by this unique capacity, which is a natural gift that cannot be learned.

The following is a selection of the statements proved most wrong by posterity.

Literature

'Sentimental rubbish . . . Show me one page that contains an idea.'

Odessa Courier on *Anna Karenina* by Leo Tolstoy, 1877

'Shakespeare's name, you may depend on it, stands absurdly too high and will go down.'

Lord Byron, 1814

'His fame is gone out like a candle in a snuff and his memory will always stink.'

William Winstanley on Milton, 1687

'It is becoming painfully obvious that Henry James has

[251]

written himself out as far as any kind of novel writing is concerned.'

William Morton Payne in 1884, before James had written *The Bostonians*, *The Turn of the Screw*, *The Ambassadors*, *What Maisie Knew*, *The Aspern Papers*, *The Golden Bowl* and most of the novels on which his reputation now rests.

'Monsieur Flaubert is not a writer.'
   Le Figaro, 1857

'Mr Waugh displays none of the elan that distinguishes the true satirist.'
   Dudley Fitts reviewing Evelyn Waugh's *Vile Bodies* in 1930

'A hundred years from now it is very likely that *The Jumping Frog* alone will be remembered.'
   Harry Thurston Peck on the works of Mark Twain, 1901

'I'm sorry, Mr Kipling, but you just don't know how to use the English language.'
   The *San Francisco Examiner*'s rejection letter to Rudyard Kipling in 1889.

'This is a book of the season only.'
   New York Herald Tribune on *The Great Gatsby* by F. Scott Fitzgerald

'Few are good for much.'

Henry Hallam on John Donne's poetry

'We do not believe in the permanence of his reputation . . . Our children will wonder what their ancestors
could have meant by putting Dickens at the head of
the novelists of his day.'

Saturday Review, 1858

'We cannot name one considerable poem of his that is
likely to remain upon the thresh-floor of Fame.'

London Weekly Review, 1828 on Samuel Taylor
Coleridge

'It would be useless to pretend that they can be very
widely read.'

Manchester Guardian on the novels of Joseph Conrad,
1902

'Chaucer, notwithstanding the praises bestowed upon
him . . . Does not deserve so well as Thomas of Ercil-
doune.'

Lord Byron, 1835

'His versification is so destitute of sustained harmony
and many of his thoughts so strained . . . that I have
always believed his verses would soon rank with forgotten things.'

John Quincy Adams on Lord Byron, 1830

'The only consolation which we have in reflecting upon it is that it will never be generally read.'

James Lorimer reviewing *Wuthering Heights* by Emily Brontë, 1847

'Monsieur de Balzac's place in French literature will be neither considerable nor high.'

Eugène Poitou in *Revue des Deux Mondes*, 1856

'In a hundred years' time the histories of French literature will only mention it as a curio.'

Emile Zola on *Les Fleurs du Mal* by Charles Baudelaire, 1857

'An endless wilderness of dull, flat, prosaic twaddle.'

T. B. Macauley on *The Prelude* by William Wordsworth

'Nothing odd will do long. *Tristram Shandy* did not last.'

Samuel Johnson in 1776 on a novel that is still in print 236 years later

'My dear fellow, I may perhaps be dead from the neck up, but rack my brains as I may I can't see why a chap should need thirty pages to describe how he turns over in bed before going to sleep.'

Marc Humbolt, a French editor, rejecting *In Remembrance of Times Past* by Marcel Proust in 1912

Music

'I would say that this does not belong to the art which I am in the habit of considering music.'

A. Oulibicheff reviewing Beethoven's Fifth Symphony.

'As a work of art, it is naught.'

The *New York Times* review of Bizet's *Carmen*, 24 October 1878

'Not only does Monsieur Berlioz not have any melodic ideas, but, when one occurs to him, he does not know how to handle it, for he does not know how to write.'

Paul Scudo, *Critique et littérature musicales*, 1852

'The art of composing without ideas has decidedly found in Brahms one of its worthiest representatives.'

Hugo Wolf, 1886

'Had he submitted this music to a teacher, the latter, it is to be hoped, would have torn it up and thrown it at his feet.'

L. Rellstab reviewing Chopin's *Mazurkas* in 1833

'Debussy's music is the dreariest kind of rubbish.'

New York Post, 22 March 1907

'Liszt is a commonplace person with his hair on end. He writes the ugliest music extant.'

Dramatic and Musical Review, London, 1843

'It is not fair to the readers of the *Musical Courier* to take up their time with a detailed description of that musical monstrosity, which masquerades under the title of Gustav Mahler's Fourth Symphony. There is nothing in the design, content or execution of the work to impress the musician.'

Musical Courier, New York, November 1904

'Devoid of all musical interest'

New York World on Prokofiev, November 1918

'Silly and inconsequential'

H. E. Krehbiel reviewing Puccini's *La Bohème* in *The New York Tribune*, 27 December 1900

'Ravel's *Boléro* I submit as the most insolent monstrosity ever perpetuated in the history of music.'

Edward Robinson, *The American Mercury*, May 1932

'The harmonies are so obtrusively crude that no number of wrong notes would be detected by the subtlest listeners.'

H. F. Chorley, on Schumann's Piano Variations (four hands)

'Vulgar, self-indulgent and provincial beyond all description.'

Virgil Thomson on Sibelius's Second Symphony in the *New York Herald Tribune*, 11 October 1940

'Strauss can be characterised in four words: little talent, much impudence.'

César Cui, 5 December 1904

'It is probable that much, if not most, of Stravinsky's music will enjoy brief existence.'

W. J. Henderson, *New York Sun*, 16 January 1937

'Tchaikovsky's First Piano Concerto, like the first pancake, is a flop.'

Nicolai Soloviev, *Novoye Vremya*, 13 November 1875

'As an opera, *Eugene Onegin* is stillborn and absolutely incompetent.'

César Cui, *Nedelya*, St Petersburg, 5 November 1884

'*Rigoletto* is the weakest work of Verdi. It lacks melody. This opera has hardly any chance of being kept in the repertoire.'

Gazette Musicale de Paris, 22 May 1853

'I scarcely think it will be able to keep the stage for any length of time.'

E. A. Kelley, reviewing Wagner's *Lohengrin*, 2 April 1854

'The musical value of this score is precisely zero.'

Echo, Berlin, No. 22, reviewing Wagner's opera *Rienzi* in 1871

'But oh, the pages of stupid and hopelessly vulgar music! The unspeakable cheapness of the chief tune . . . Do you believe way down in the bottom of your heart that if this music had been written by Mr John L. Tarbox, now living in Sandown, New Hampshire, any conductor here or in Europe could be persuaded to put it in rehearsal?'

Philip Hale on Beethoven's Ninth Symphony in the *Musical Record*, Boston, 1 June 1899

'Brahms evidently lacks the breadth and power of invention eminently necessary for the production of truly great symphonic work.'

Musical Courier, New York, 1887

'Who has heard *that*, and finds it beautiful, is beyond help.'

Eduard Hanslik on Liszt's B minor Sonata, 1881

'Beethoven always sounds to me like the upsetting of bags of nails, with here and there an also dropped hammer.'

John Ruskin, 6 February 1881

'Sure-fire rubbish'

Lawrence Gilman, reviewing *Porgy and Bess* by George Gershwin in the *New York Herald Tribune*, 1935

'Far too noisy, my dear Mozart. Far too many notes.'

The Emperor Joseph II after the first performance of
Die Entführung aus dem Serail

'If Beethoven's Seventh Symphony is not by some
means abridged, it will soon fall into disuse.'

Philip Hale, Boston music critic, 1837

'I played over the music of that scoundrel Brahms. What
a giftless bastard! It annoys me that this self-inflated
mediocrity is hailed as a genius. Why, in comparison
with him, Raff is a genius.'

Tchaikovsky's diary, 9 October 1886

'We don't like their sound. Groups of guitars are on the
way out.'

Decca Recording Company when turning down the
Beatles in 1962. (The group was also turned down by
Pye, Colombia and HMV.)

Everything Else

'Sterility may be inherited.'
Pacific Rural News

'The Olympic Games can no more have a deficit than a
man can have a baby.'

Mayor Jean Drapeau of Montreal three weeks before

the 1976 Olympics, as a result of which his city lost one billion dollars

'Rembrandt is not to be compared in the painting of character with our own extraordinarily gifted English artist, Mr Rippingille.'
    John Hunt (1775–1848)

'Flight by machines heavier than air is unpractical and insignificant, if not utterly impossible.'
    Simon Newcomb (1835–1909). The first flight by the Wright brothers eighteen months afterwards did not affect his opinion.

'Heaven and earth were created all together in the same instant, on October 23rd, 4004 BC at nine o'clock in the morning.'
    Dr John Lightfoot, Vice Chancellor of Cambridge University, just before the publication of Darwin's *Origin of Species*

'Rail travel at high speed is not possible because passengers, unable to breathe, would die of asphyxia.'
    Dr Dionysys Lardner (1793–1859), Professor of Natural Philosophy and Astronomy at University College, London. He also asserted that no large steamship would ever be able to cross the Atlantic, since it would require more coal than it could carry. Two years later the *Great Western* crossed the Atlantic.

'Animals, which move, have limbs and muscles. The earth does not have limbs and muscles; therefore it does not move.'

Scipio Chiaramonti

'Stanley Matthews lacks the big-match temperament. He will never hold down a regular first-team place in top-class soccer.'

Unsigned football writer when Matthews, the future captain of England, made his debut at the age of seventeen

'I can accept the theory of relativity as little as I can accept the existence of atoms and other such dogmas.'

Ernst Mach (1838–1916), Professor of Physics at the University of Vienna

'The energy produced by the breaking down of the atom is a very poor kind of thing. Anyone who expects a source of power from the transformation of these atoms is talking moonshine.'

Ernest Rutherford (1871–1937) after he had split the atom for the first time

'You will never amount to very much.'

A Munich schoolmaster to Albert Einstein, aged ten

'ALL THE PASSENGERS ARE SAFE'

Lancashire Evening Post headline on its report of the *Titanic* sinking

'DEWEY DEFEATS TRUMAN'

Chicago Tribune headline on November 1948 after the convincing re-election of President Truman to office

'Television won't last. It's a flash in the pan.'

Mary Somerville, pioneer of radio educational broadcasts, 1948

'If the Earth did move, how could we keep a grip on it with our feet? We could walk only very, very slowly; and should find it slipping rapidly under our footsteps. Then, which way is it turning? If we walked in the direction of its tremendous speed, it would push us on terribly rapidly. But if we tried to walk against its revolving . . .? Either way we should be terribly giddy, and our digestive process impossible.'

Margaret Missen, *The Sun Goes Round the Earth*

'You care for nothing but shooting, dogs and rat-catching and you will be a disgrace to yourself and all your family.'

Charles Darwin's father reviewing his son's academic prospects

'The moon has a coating of ice 140 miles thick.'

Hans Hörbiger, World Ice Theory proponent, 1913

'Everything that can be invented has been invented.'

The Director of the US Patent Office in 1899

'Unworthy of the attention of practical or scientific men'

The conclusion of a parliamentary committee's report on whether Edison's electric light bulb would ever be relevant to Britain

'Democracy will be dead by 1950.'

John Langton-Davies, *A Short History of the Future*, 1936

'There is no likelihood man can ever tap the power of the atom.'

Dr Robert Mullikan, 1923 Nobel Prize winner

'In all likelihood world inflation is over.'

Managing Director of the International Monetary Fund, 1959

'Very interesting, Whittle, my boy, but it will never work.'

The Professor of Aeronautical Engineering at Cambridge University when shown Frank Whittle's plan for the jet engine

'I make bold to say that I don't believe that in the future history of the world any such feat will be performed by anybody else.'

The Mayor of Dover in 1875 after Matthew Webb had swum the English Channel

Lord Kelvin: A Special Tribute

'Radio has no future.'

Lord Kelvin, President of the Royal Society, 1890–95

'Heavier-than-air flying machines are impossible.'

Lord Kelvin, President of the Royal Society, 1890–95

'X-rays will prove to be a hoax.'

Lord Kelvin, President of the Royal Society, 1890–95

And, of Course

'There are too many books. I shall never write one.'

Stephen Pile, December 1977, who wrote three books on the subject of heroic failure before falling for ever silent upon the topic thirty-two years later

EPILOGUE

Farewell Address

Today I lay down my field marshal's baton and say farewell to a lifelong topic. I have written my last ever word on the subject of heroic failure. This is goodbye, troops.

Of course, I will never lose interest in this great subject and even now at the eleventh hour I was excited to hear this week about the man who wrote to *The Times* every day for thirty-five years without ever having a letter published, the robbers who forgot to put petrol in their getaway car and asked their victim for a push, and the illustrious Robert 'Choc' Thornton, our most accident-prone jockey, who has fallen off his horse a record 367 times. Speaking from his hospital bed, he said, 'I haven't thought about giving up.' Of course not. The whole idea is preposterous.

Before I say goodbye, troops, may I tell you how it began and how it ended?

This is how it began.

It was 1957 and yoghurt was still some way off.

One night I was taken to see the Luton Girls' Grammar School production of *A Midsummer Night's Dream*. It was all right (lovers and fairies), but, oh, the rude mechanicals' play. If anything could enter the soul of a 1950s Luton schoolboy this did.

When Bottom the Weaver staged his divinely inept, exquisitely amateur and breathtakingly dreadful *Tragedy of Pyramus and Thisbe* without any of the theatrical skills normally required for this endeavour, he and his friends stole the show. Forget the lovers and the fairies. This was it.

In that moment I realised that doing something badly could, in the right hands, be much more impressive than merely doing it well.

This required a special talent, a lateral vision, a panache, style and skill that amounted to genius. It liberated us from the restrictive shackles of conventional expectation and explored whole scales and registers of human potential that were surreal and utterly life-enhancing. As Tolstoy very nearly said, 'All successful people are the same, but everyone who messes up big time does so in a way that is unique and completely individual.'

Watching the rude mechanicals, I felt a glow that came from a combination of laughter and affection. I have felt that same glow for thirty-two years every time I came across a story of heroic failure.

Three decades later yoghurt is the norm and I have now written three volumes, acclaiming the worst in every sphere.

In 1979 the first *Book of Heroic Failures* was written with the flow of the culture. It was like shouting into a cave and the echo that came back was louder than my original cry. The British knew in their heart and in their soul what this was about. It was part of our national character. (The Irish echo was even louder and no part of the world seemed entirely impervious to this simple idea, all bar America, which stared glum and unsmiling at the whole notion, lassoed as they were to their American Dream.)

Then in 1980 Margaret Thatcher said, 'Britain is a country dedicated to success, not failure.'

I decided to lie low. I still went on collecting these stories, like an underground resistance fighter, because ever since she said this we have lived through a golden age.

The record for the most callouts of a lifeboat during a single voyage is up from four to a monumental eleven, thanks to Eric 'the Navigator' Abbott. The most attempts to murder a spouse without him realising there is a problem is up to seven and Mrs Cha Sa-soon has broken the world record for the most failures of the driving test with a personal best of 959.

When Mrs Thatcher said that, it was not actually true. We were nuts about Eddie 'the Eagle' Edwards, who entered the Olympic ski jump having been on skis only two or three times at a dry slope outside Cheltenham. His glasses steamed up on take-off and he wasn't allowed into his own press conference because he did not have the right credentials. The British rose up in his honour.

But thirty years later things had changed. I knew I was in trouble when I watched *Match of the Day*. On came Mick McCarthy, the manager of Wolverhampton Wanderers. 'I don't believe in this heroic failure,' he said. 'You've got to win.'

Mick McCarthy was eventually sacked after a fabulous 5–1 home defeat to West Bromwich Albion. And that is the whole point. If success could be guaranteed by hard work and good intentions, I would be all for it, but a lot goes wrong on this planet; few can win, and as a species we live close to disaster so we need a philosophical attitude.

In 2011 the third, final and *Ultimate Book of Heroic Failures* was written against the flow of the culture.

Today I even detect a slight reluctance to use the term 'heroic failure' at all. A Sunday newspaper ran two pages of extracts from this book without once employing the expression. The headline was 'Epic Failures'.

Well, epic failure is not the same thing. It removes the heroic status of the person messing up and concentrates on the scale of the mess. There seems to be a reluctance to ascribe heroism to failure even as a joke. We are all Americans now.

In interviews I stopped saying 'all successful people are the same' because I noticed that interviewers got twitchy and did not know how to react in this age of *The X-Factor* and *The Apprentice* where success is all.

Of the thirteen local radio stations who wanted to talk about *The Ultimate Book of Heroic Failures*, not one was south of Northampton or east of Salisbury (the

Irish have also dropped off the map, tragically in my view). Of those thirteen, the older interviewers were straight there and nothing had changed, but some of the younger ones needed the whole idea explaining to them. 'Why have you written a book laughing at losers?' one young interviewer said.

I explained to this young man that they are not losers and I am not laughing at them. I am singing their praises and my attitude comes from my parents' wartime generation. It was a make-the-best-of-a-bad-job, smiling-through, that's-life attitude that meant they could go to Dunkirk in small rickety boats to perform acts of quiet heroism without health and safety stopping them. It was the sane counsel of imperfection

He had no idea what I was talking about.

In fact, heroic failure now finds itself in the same position as the FA Cup.

When I was a boy Third Division Norwich City knocked mighty Manchester United out of the Cup in the sixth round. It reverberated for decades as one of the great acts of giant-killing because the FA Cup embodied the principle of the Levellers and the Diggers in the English Civil War – that the 'least he' is as worthy of respect as the 'greatest he'.

Nowadays such a victory would attract a good crowd and amuse us for a week or so, but it would not deflect us from our real interest. Will mighty Manchester United beat mighty Barcelona or moneybags Manchester City in the Champion's League?

Today we are more impressed by Goliath than we are by David.

This means that I have spent thirty-two years writing three books, persuading the world that success is over-rated, while the world has hurtled ever faster in exactly the opposite direction.

That is as it should be. The result is that I am the least influential author on the planet and have now earned a place in my own book.

This is how it ended.

Goodbye, troops. You're on your own now. Stand easy.

Also by Stephen Pile

THE ULTIMATE BOOK OF HEROIC FAILURES

The *Sunday Times* Humour Book of the Year

These are the all-time greats, Gods in the field of failure, surreal artists, who spurn mere drab success to explore the vast, magical, life-enhancing possibilities of getting it wrong.

From the most driving test failures (959), to the most pointless election (in Dakota, in which not even the mayor voted), the worst robbery (when two different sets of bank robbers struck simultaneously) and the worst mugger (who left his victim $250 better off), to the holidaying rugby team of fifty-somethings from Dorchester who, due to a mistranslation, ended up playing the top team from Romania live on state TV, this is the ultimate book to make you feel better about yourself and the world around you.

'Packed with lots of new, wonderful true stories of disaster, idiocy and sheer bad luck.' Simon Hoggart, *Guardian*

www.faber.co.uk

ff

FABER
MEMBERS

Become a Faber Member
and discover the best in
the arts and literature.

Sign up to the Faber Members programme
and enjoy specially curated events, tailored
discounts, and exclusive previews of our
forthcoming publications from the best
novelists, poets, playwrights, thinkers,
musicians and artists.

Join for free today at faber.co.uk/members

ff